THE MILITARY MONEY MANUAL

THE MILITARY MONEY MANUAL

A PRACTICAL GUIDE TO FINANCIAL FREEDOM

SPENCER C. REESE

Production & Art Direction: Saeah Wood
Editing: Adam M. Rosen & Saeah Wood
Design & Layout: Bohdan Skubko

With Special Thanks to Beta Readers:
Adam Dunne, Kate Horrell, James Leenman, Doug Nordman,
Ryan Walsh, Samantha Saldivar, Sebastian Saldivar,
& Connor Muilenburg.

Hardcover 978-1-955671-04-0
Paperback 978-1-955671-05-7
E-Book 978-1-955671-06-4
Audiobook 978-1-955671-07-1

otterpine.com   militarymoneymanual.com

CONTENTS

NOTE FROM THE AUTHOR

Thank you for picking up this book. By doing so, you've taken the first step towards earning *your* financial freedom.

This book is meant to be short and to the point. You can read it in a single afternoon, but I hope that it acts as a companion on your own journey towards financial independence (FI). You can find additional information and resources on the topics I cover at the end of the book.

I was commissioned through Air Force ROTC in 2010 after four years of college. I graduated with an economics degree. I had an interest in finance from a young age, but I started studying it in depth during the global financial crisis of 2008. Since then, I have invested thousands of hours studying, researching, and applying investing and personal finance principles to my own life. In 2012, I started writing about FI, personal finance, investing, and travel hacking on my website, militarymoneymanual.com.

I was once a brand-new officer in the US military, unsure of how to invest my money. Like many Americans, I graduated college with over $60,000 in student loan debt. But by the time I made captain four years later, I had paid off my debt, bought and sold my first house, and saved a six-figure net worth.

I made some mistakes along the way, but I earned much more than I lost. In this book, I share that hard-won knowledge with you.

This book can give you the tools to become a successful investor and achieve financial freedom. I hope to show you that the best financial goal worth pursuing is financial independence.

If you have any questions, please visit my website and fill out the contact form or send me an email at spencer@ militarymoneymanual.com. Introduce yourself or ask me a question. I'd love to hear your story and learn from you. Best of luck in your investing endeavors!

IF YOU DON'T HAVE TIME TO READ ANYTHING ELSE

Take a deep breath. Then just do this (in this order):

1. Start a monthly 5 percent contribution of your military base pay to your Roth Thrift Savings Plan (TSP).

2. Create a TSP account and ensure you are invested in the latest "L Fund" closest to your retirement date.

3. To start, save $1,000 for an emergency fund.

4. Budget a realistic amount for rent, food, transportation, and other expenses.

5. Pay down high-interest-rate debts.

6. Based on your budget, increase your emergency fund to cover three months of expenses.

7. Open a Vanguard Roth individual retirement account (IRA) and contribute the maximum annual limit to the Vanguard Total Stock Market Index Fund (VTSAX).

8. Max out your Roth TSP contributions annually.

9. Build the life you want and then save for it.

10. Save enough to rapidly achieve financial independence. A 50 percent savings rate can mean financial independence in 17 years.

If you want more details on how to execute these steps, keep reading. We'll get deeper into investing strategies and principles you can use to rapidly achieve financial independence.

You can read this book straight through, and you can review each individual chapter as needed. Each chapter builds on knowledge from the previous ones.

INTRODUCTION

This is the book I wish someone had handed me on my first day in the military. As a college graduate and commissioned second lieutenant in the United States Air Force, I had no idea what to do with the money the US government sent my way on the 1st and 15th of every month.

Whether officer or enlisted, active or reserve, you might be like I was not too many years ago: new to the military and completely confused about what to do with your money. You may recall hearing about the "TSP" or a "Roth IRA"—whatever they are—and think that saving 10 percent of your income is a decent goal.

But no one has explained what the endgame is. What's the point of all of this saving? Allow me to show you what the endgame looks like, and why it matters—a lot. I'll show you what I did with my money to set myself up for long-term financial success and how you can do the same.

When you're young, you lay the financial foundation for the rest of your life. The choices you make when you're young—whether you invest, accumulate debt, or just let life happen—will impact you for the rest of your life. If you have kids, those decisions may impact your family for decades.

Collecting a paycheck after being a student can be incredibly liberating. But if you're not smart about it, that money can quickly disappear. Cars, rent, food, taxes, toys, video games, beer, haircuts, cell phones—the list goes on and on. Everybody is clamoring to get their hands on your dollars, but you need to pay yourself first. Discipline now will lead to more financial freedom in the future.

I grew up reading articles in the magazines *Forbes*, *Fortune*, and *Money*. I saved my summer job money and bought the SPY ETF (a popular S&P 500 exchange-traded fund) in the Roth IRA my dad helped me open. Despite my youthful interest in investing, I was financially literate but not financially competent. The financial magazines and news outlets offered lots of questionable tactics but no strategy. I knew I should save, invest, and minimize credit card debt, but I was confused about how much I needed to save.

After I entered the military and started earning a regular paycheck, I was still confused. I knew the power of compounding interest would someday turn my summer savings into millions, but when? How long would those millions last if I wanted to stop working? Would I have to work forever? Or was there a finish line to eventually cross?

Retirement was so far away. How on earth was I going to save the money I would need to retire comfortably? How could I possibly figure out my retirement "number" (the amount of money it would take to be financially free)? Was it half a million dollars? One million? Two million? I couldn't figure out how to connect the dots.

On top of this confusion, at the time, a quarter of my after-tax pay went towards student loan repayments. I couldn't figure out how to get rid of the debt quickly. I had heard about the military's Thrift Savings Plan (TSP), but I didn't know if it was a good place to invest my money.

I had all these questions, and no one in my chain of command offered any answers. No one explained how money worked and how it could work for me. No one explained why I should go through the hassle of learning how to become rich. It was all theoretical. I still didn't understand what the endgame was.

That's why I wrote this book: to provide you with the direction I wish someone had given me when I joined the military.

DO YOU WANT TO WORK FOREVER?

Ask yourself: "Do you want to work forever?" Or would you rather have enough invested money and/or passive income to make work a choice instead of a necessity?

How good would it feel to wake up every morning and think, "If I quit my job today, I wouldn't have to worry about bills. I could walk away and never work another day in my life. I have no debts. My car, home, and student loans are paid off. I can live off my investments for the rest of my life. I choose to work because I love helping people and because it brings me joy."

When you get to this point, you can travel the world, raise your kids at home, visit family and friends whenever you want, work out on your own schedule, cook delicious and healthy meals at home, read for half the morning, and take naps in the afternoons. You'll have time to meet friends for coffee and time to start the homebrewing project that's been on your list for years. You can work because you want to without worrying about promoting, networking, selling, or doing any of the things that you hate doing. You can tell your boss "no" and not worry about the consequences.

Does that sound awesome? Of course! Does it sound realistic? Probably not if you are sweating it out in a desert on deployment. But this plan *is* realistic. Thousands have already achieved it. You can achieve this financial position much sooner than you think.

MY WAKE-UP CALL

I stumbled my way through that first year on a military paycheck. I was in a year-long training course working my ass off, and I struggled to make it through each day. My only goal was to not wash out, so I didn't make time to think about my finances.

During that year of training, I made no progress against my student loan debts, and I didn't build any assets. Every paycheck gave me just enough money to get to the next paycheck but never enough to get ahead. Luckily, I didn't accumulate any credit card debt, but I didn't have much to show after a year of work.

After completing the training course, I finally had a few weeks off. I spent more time reading personal finance blogs online, and I went to a local library and checked out every book they had on personal finance.

Finally, it clicked. Reading a few of the classic personal finance books like *The Millionaire Next Door*, *Personal Finance for Dummies*, and *The Total Money Makeover* provided the wake-up call I needed! I understood what I should do with the money Uncle Sam paid me. I realized this money wasn't just for "present me"—it was also for "future me." With the right strategy, I could make my money work for me and eventually liberate myself from needing a job to support my lifestyle.

I realized what the point of all this saving and investing was: financial independence.

FINANCIAL INDEPENDENCE

Financial independence. I heard this phrase for the first time a couple years after I commissioned. If only someone had told me about it when I was a cadet in Air Force ROTC!

Financial independence (FI) occurs when your assets and/or passive income can provide enough income to cover your lifestyle expenses. Assets appreciate or gain value over time, like real estate, stocks, and bonds. Lifestyle expenses are the basic recurring expenses of life such as housing, food, and transportation. They also include expenses like travel, hobbies, entertainment, and anything else you spend money on to enrich your life. If your annual expenses are $50,000 and you have $1,000,000 invested in a way that provides a 5 percent annual return, you are financially independent ($1,000,000 x 5% = $50,000/year).

Unfortunately, we live in the real world, where you have an insidious threat called inflation which is always working against you. Inflation is the natural rise of prices in a growing economy. Inflation is the reason a gallon of milk is $5 now when it was $1 in the 1960s. You must buy assets that grow faster than inflation or your savings will slowly become worth less every year. (We'll cover specific assets to invest in later in the book.)

Let's assume you've invested your money diligently for 20 years. You now have $1 million invested in stocks, bonds, and other assets. How much of that money can you spend every year and not run out before you die?

In 1998, three professors at Trinity University in San Antonio, Texas studied this exact question. Their work became known as the "Trinity Study." The professors looked at each 30-year period in the stock market from 1926 to 1995. From this data, they came up with a number called the safe withdrawal rate or SWR.

SWR is the percentage of money someone can withdraw from their total investment portfolio while maintaining a survival rate of greater than 95 percent for more than 30 years. Survival rate here means that after 30 years of annual withdrawals, one would have at least $1 left in his or her portfolio.

The original Trinity Study found 3–4 percent as a very safe withdrawal rate, especially for stock-dominated portfolios. This became known as the "4 percent rule."

There is some debate on how low your withdrawal rate should be to be considered safe. With nearly 25 more years of data since the Trinity Study, financial nerds on the internet have further refined the SWR. You can run your own safe withdrawal rate calculations on different sites such as networthify.com, engaging-data.com, or firecalc.com.

But even today, most experts seem to agree that the ideal SWR number is still between 3–4 percent, depending on how long you want the money to last, what you are invested in, and how much risk you want to take.

If you have a $1 million portfolio, you can withdraw 3–4 percent of your portfolio and pay yourself $30,000–$40,000 per year for the rest of your life, assuming your portfolio is stock-heavy.

Expressed another way, the 3–4 percent withdrawal rate can become a goal. Take the inverse of 3–4 percent, and you get 25x–33x. If your assets are 25–33 times your annual expenses, you are financially independent.

For example, if your annual expenses are $40,000, you need somewhere between $1–$1.32 million to be safely financially independent, based on a 3–4 percent SWR. This formula works at any spending level. Whatever lifestyle you want, just multiply the annual expenses for that lifestyle by 25 or 33 to arrive at your goal number for FI.

Here is a table for example lifestyles:

Monthly Expenses	Annual Expenses	FI Number at 25x	FI Number at 33x
$2,000	$24,000	$600,000	$792,000
$3,333	$40,000	$1,000,000	$1,320,000
$5,000	$60,000	$1,500,000	$1,980,000
$8,333	$100,000	$2,500,000	$3,300,000
$10,000	$120,000	$3,000,000	$3,960,000

Don't worry too much about the difference between 25x and 33x your annual expenses. Focus on the 25x number to start and continue to learn about safe withdrawal rates as you build your net worth over the years.

If you have a military or government pension or another source of retirement income such as Social Security, you can reduce your annual expenses by your expected income, which will reduce the amount you must save. Using the 4 percent rule, if your military pension covers $20,000 per year, you can reduce the amount you need to save by $500,000.

So that's the goal, expressed in a single, simple number. If you want to be financially independent, you need your invested assets to be between 25 and 33 times your annual expenses.

Depending on your lifestyle and the amount you can save, I believe that you can achieve FI within 10–20 years of reading this book. To achieve FI, all that's required is a bit of work, some simple investing, and time.

After thousands of hours of reading, studying, writing, thinking, and investing, I continue to come back to the simple conclusion that FI is the ultimate financial goal worth pursuing. How long you take to get there, or if you get there at all, is up to you.

That said, I want you to consider what FI will bring to your life. What is the point of becoming financially independent? Why spend time reading this book? Why take the time to learn a bit about investments? Why bother to set up an automatic investment plan?

I have one simple answer to those questions: freedom. That's the point of all this work. That's what the endgame is. When you are financially independent, you no longer need to work for money. Money now works for you. That gives you choice. Choices provide freedom, and freedom ultimately brings happiness.

FINANCIAL INDEPENDENCE: WHAT IT MEANS FOR YOU

Financial independence is flexible. The FI finish line is completely defined by you. Through your savings rate, you choose when you become FI. Through the amount you save, you decide what lifestyle you want to live post-FI.

There are many versions of FI but here are three examples: lean FI, regular FI, and fat FI.

- **Lean FI** is when you achieve a savings amount that would support the minimum viable lifestyle you want to live. Depending on where you live, that could be very low. For example, in Southeast Asia, expats can live comfortably on as little as $12,000 per year. That would require $300,000 in savings based on the 4 percent rule.

- **Regular FI** is when you can sustain your current lifestyle based on your invested assets. For example, in 2020, the median annual expenses in the US was about $60,000 per year which would require $1,500,000 in savings based on the 4 percent rule.

- **Fat FI** is saving for an extravagant lifestyle, like one that spends six figures a year. People with fat FIs typically have a net worth of $5 million or more (or at least should!), which can support annual expenses of $200,000 per year and higher.

These categories of FI are just made up. There is no FI police.

If your regular lifestyle costs you $100,000 per year and you want to keep living it, $2.5M should be enough savings to support it. That doesn't mean you are in a fat FI. You don't need to label your lifestyle.

FI is all about choices and freedom. As you move up the FI ladder, you can jump off at any point or get back on and keep climbing. You may achieve regular FI and decide to keep working and saving while dedicating any additional income to exciting vacations with your loved ones or additional charitable donations.

Alternatively, you may achieve regular FI and decide that, at your current spending level, you are happy with what you have. Why keep working at a job you don't like when there are more important things to do? You can step off the career ladder and explore the world for a bit.

The choice is yours!

WHAT'S THE POINT OF FI?

So what's the point of saving and investing all this money? Why not just spend more than 90 percent of your income and invest hardly anything like many others?

For me, it's all about freedom. Freedom to choose how I work, where I work, and what I work on. Freedom to choose how I spend my time. Freedom to choose between having no children or having seven.

For you, it may be about creating a better life for your family, funding your children's college educations, retiring to that lake house, or living the rich life of your dreams. FI is a personal choice and requires personal motivation to achieve it.

Being smart about your financial choices isn't just about saving and investing, but also about making choices about money that align with your values and the things you love. Most things that bring you joy and satisfaction probably come with extra costs. That could be a trip to Cambodia, an expensive car, your love of scuba diving, or having a big family.

So take some time to find the why behind your FI, so you can make smart choices for you and your family.

If you're happy to work the 0730–1630 every day for the rest of your life, that's fine. Do what makes you happy. But make the conscious choice. Don't keep living life on autopilot.

I believe that many people do not realize how unhappy they are with their current financial situation until they start analyzing and asking the big questions like:

- What is the point of working?

- Do I want to work forever?

- Will I have to work until I earn a military pension or even worse, until I'm 70?

- If I had $20,000,000 and could quit working tomorrow, what would I do with my time?

Financial independence is a state of freedom that most people only dream about. But it is achievable. Many military and civilian workers have done it.

When you no longer have to work for money, you can work on the things that bring you the most happiness. I know that when I achieve FI, I will continue to work on the things I love. Things I'm looking forward to post-FI include educating my readers through my website, running with my dog, and planning our next around-the-world travel adventure.

If you follow the advice in this book for the next 15-20 years, you can easily achieve FI. If you have a spouse that shares your dream of FI, you will get there even faster, especially if he or she brings in additional income.

Note that if two spouses earn the same amount of money, if you save one person's income, you are already at a 50 percent savings rate. Rapid FI is much easier to obtain with a strong partner by your side.

FINANCIAL INDEPENDENCE GAME PLAN

Here's a checklist you can use to become financially independent in less than 20 years. It's simple—only nine steps—and if you can internalize them and apply the principles, you will get there.

1. Avoid high-interest-rate debt.

2. Set up a Roth TSP account and begin contributing 5 percent of your base pay.

3. Ensure your TSP allocation is in a Lifecycle Fund.

4. Do not buy an expensive new car. Stick with a reliable used car.

5. Be amazing and proficient at your job, learn your trade, and work at being the best you can be.

6. Read a few books and blogs about FI. If it's what you want, make it a priority in your life.

7. Ramp up your investing rate to a minimum of 45 percent to achieve FI in less than 20 years.

8. Max out your TSP and IRA contributions and invest the leftover cash in a taxable investment account.

9. Always have your endgame in sight. When your annual expenses multiplied by 25 equals your invested net worth, you have achieved financial independence!

FI will not take forever. The point at which you reach FI is merely a function of time, investment return, and savings rate. The most important factor within your control is your savings rate, which I discuss in more detail in the next chapter. If you can save 80 percent of your income (e.g. live on $40,000/year while making $200,000/year), you can be FI in six years, assuming a 6 percent real rate of return. Just five years of working and you can be done!

You choose how quickly you achieve FI and how extravagant your lifestyle is. You decide when you want to be free from needing a paycheck. Whether it is five years from now, 15 years, or never, your savings rate and investments determine when you will become FI.

One of my favorite thought experiments when visualizing FI is this: every $1,000 you cut from your annual expenses is $25,000 less you need to save to reach FI. Based on the 4 percent rule, you need 25x your annual expenses invested to be FI. Thus $1,000 in expenses cut x 25 = $25,000.

I have heard that some service members save 90 percent or more of their paycheck while they are deployed. Even when at home in garrison, many service members can save 20, 30, or 40 percent of their paychecks. Once you begin cutting out the wasteful spending in your budget and focus on paying yourself first, saving money becomes easier.

As your time in service increases and you get promoted, your base pay and basic allowance for housing or BAH will increase. Don't let lifestyle inflation eat away at your increased pay. It's amazing how once you have a good home, a decent car, a few hobbies, and good food, spending more money does not increase your happiness very much. Rather than focusing on material things, put that extra income to work for you and achieve FI more quickly.

Defy the common advice and be a super saver. The more you can save and invest in low-cost passive index funds, the quicker you will achieve FI.

You have a choice with every dollar you earn: spend it now or invest it and get just a little bit closer to FI. You have this power—it's within your control. Don't let anyone tell you it's not possible. I did it and so can you.

STARTING EARLY MATTERS

I can't overstate the importance of starting your investing habit early. As an example, consider Amanda, Bill, and Chris. They all invest in their TSP Lifecycle Fund, which I discuss in more detail in the chapter "Investing While Serving in the Military" and receive a 7 percent average return over their lives.

- Amanda invests $5,000 per year from age 20–60.

- Bill invests $5,000 per year from age 20–30 then lets the money grow without additional contributions.

- Chris gets a late start and starts investing $5,000 per year from age 30–60.

You can see from the chart that the differences in gains are enormous.

STARTING EARLY MATTERS

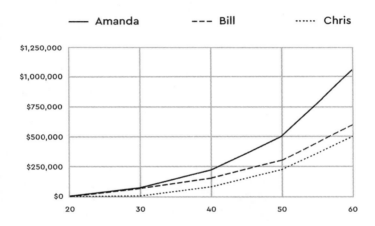

All invest in the latest TSP Lifecycle Fund and earn an average 7% return

Age	Amanda	Bill	Chris
20	$5,000	$5,000	$0
30	$78,918	$78,918	$5,000
40	$224,326	$155,244	$78,918
50	$510,365	$305,388	$224,326
60	$1,073,048	$600,744	$510,365

The takeaway in this example is simple but alarming: the cost of delaying investing by 10 years is over half a million dollars. So do your future self a favor and start now. But remember, a high-savings rate can overcome a late start. It's never too late to start.

The best time to start investing was yesterday. The next best time is today.

NINE PRINCIPLES TO ACHIEVE
FINANCIAL INDEPENDENCE

After over a decade of deep financial research and personal investing, I've distilled everything I've learned about money down to these nine principles. These are the exact principles I used to achieve financial independence (FI) before I turned 40.

These ideas are timeless and apply to all financial situations. Think of them as the "Nine Commandments" of personal finance. They apply even in seemingly unique situations such as financial catastrophes, medical issues, or overwhelming debt. The principles are the same, no matter what age or rank you are:

1. Spend less than you earn.

2. Avoid debt.

3. Pay down your high-interest-rate debt ASAP.

4. Save a three-month emergency fund.

5. Maximize your tax-advantaged retirement account contributions.

6. Remember that savings rate beats investment return.

7. Keep your investments low-cost, automatic, diversified, and simple (LADS).

8. Spend your money on what matters most to you.

9. Buy income-producing assets, not liabilities.

PRINCIPLE ONE:
SPEND LESS THAN YOU EARN

If you spend more than you earn, you are never going to get ahead. You must set aside a portion of your income for investments if you ever want to achieve FI. If you want to rapidly achieve FI, a higher savings rate like 50 percent can get you there much faster.

Spending more than you earn is a recipe for credit card debt, stress, and a life of living paycheck to paycheck. You'll constantly be one financial misfortune away from disaster. There is a reason even millionaire athletes, real estate gurus, and actors go broke—they spend like billionaires. You can find ways to outspend at any income level.

There's a great quote in the book *David Copperfield* about spending less than you earn:

Annual income twenty pounds, annual expenditure nineteen nineteen and six, result happiness. Annual income twenty pounds, annual expenditure twenty pounds ought and six, result misery.

The difference between happiness and misery can be just a few dollars. The greater the difference between your fixed costs and your income, the more flexibility you have in your spending. Spend less than you earn and invest the difference.

PRINCIPLE TWO:
AVOID DEBT

Debt means that your money isn't really yours. Someone else gets a say in where your paycheck goes. When you carry debt, every paycheck you receive first belongs to your lenders, and you get the scraps. When you must pay your creditors, you delay investing in your own assets. In other words, you make them rich and delay your own FI.

The only smart debt is an asset-backed debt like a mortgage, which is a loan for real estate, and even then, it's only smart in certain scenarios. With a mortgage, you're purchasing a potentially appreciating real asset that may produce an income if you rent out the property.

Like many Americans, I graduated college with $60,000 in student loans and a USAA Career Starter Loan, a low-interest loan offered to soon-to-commission officers. Even though both of those loans are low-interest, the days I paid off these debts were extremely liberating. I strongly recommend you prioritize rapidly wiping out all your debt first. Then, focus on growing your investments.

The worst offender when it comes to debt is credit card debt or payday loan debt. The interest rates on credit card debts are often in the double digits.

Credit card debt is an insidious threat against your financial success. Always pay the full statement amount on your credit card bills. Never carry a balance from month-to-month and don't just make the minimum payments.

Payday loans are short-term loans that give you cash today for a paycheck you'll receive in a few days or weeks. These loans usually come with "service fees" and extremely high-interest rates that can mean you're paying more than 100 percent interest on a loan that lasts one to two weeks.

Payday loans are a trap many service members fall into in order to make ends meet between paychecks. Create breathing space in your budget. Consider what you can live without. This gets back to the first principle of spending less than you earn.

Auto loans are another debt trap for many young service members. They can be okay especially early in your career when you don't have much savings. If you use a low-interest rate auto loan to buy a cheap, reliable car and pay the loan off, it's not a terrible financial decision. But don't buy an expensive car with an auto loan simply because you can afford the monthly payment. We'll cover buying your first car later in the book.

PRINCIPLE THREE:
PAY DOWN HIGH-INTEREST-RATE DEBT ASAP

High-interest-rate debt destroys any financial goal, especially financial independence. Just like compounding interest works in your favor when you invest, it works just as hard against you when you owe high-interest-rate debt.

As a rule of thumb, treat any interest rate above 6 percent as high-interest debt. This is the maximum rate lenders can charge active-duty military service members for any debt they incurred before joining the military.

If you acquired debt before joining military service that is over 6 percent interest, contact the lender and inform them of your active duty military status. The lender is required by law to reduce your interest rate to 6 percent or less to comply with the Servicemembers Civil Relief Act (SCRA). The SCRA is a federal law passed by Congress in 2003.

If you have a debt over 6 percent, you must pay it off quickly. You can treat mortgage debt or any debt with a rate below 6 percent as slightly less of an emergency, but by paying it off early, you can save thousands of dollars.

Many new military investors wonder if they should prioritize debt repayment or investments. Again, if the debt is over 6 percent, focus on repaying the debt versus increasing your investment contributions. Once the debt is paid off, increase your savings rate.

The only caveat to this rule is if you are in the military's Blended Retirement System (BRS). If you are in BRS, always contribute at least 5 percent to your TSP to receive the match you're entitled to and attack your debt with your remaining funds. We'll cover BRS and the TSP in a later chapter.

Once your debt is repaid, send whatever you were paying towards your debt to your future self by contributing an equal or greater amount to your TSP.

There are two primary ways to pay off debt rapidly: the "debt snowball" and the "debt avalanche." In my experience, both methods work well. In a debt snowball, you pay off your debts in order from smallest to largest. This gives you the psychological boost of crossing them off one by one. As you pay off the smaller debts, you can direct the payments you were making towards the larger ones. If debt is a behavioral problem for you, it may help to see the small "wins."

With the debt avalanche, you pay off your highest-interest-rate debt first, as this is financially optimal. However, if your highest-interest-rate debt is your largest, you won't get the small victories along the way.

Another option is to combine the two approaches. For example, first pay off your smallest debt to prove you can do it, then move on to your loans with the highest interest rates.

It doesn't matter which tactic you use. The important thing is to become debt-free as soon as possible. If you're not sure, pick a tactic and start moving in the right direction. Pay off your debt quickly and move on to bigger financial goals.

PRINCIPLE FOUR:
SAVE A THREE-MONTH EMERGENCY FUND

Life is unpredictable, but it is predictably unpredictable. Things will break on your car, you will have random emergencies, and you will need a last-minute plane ticket back home for something. All these crises cost money, and if you don't have a dedicated emergency fund, you will constantly stumble from one emergency to the next.

To smooth out life's bumps, start by saving $1,000 as fast as you can. Then work towards saving three months of expenses in cash. Whether this is three months of your basic expenses (food, housing, transportation) or three months of all your expenses (adding the subscription entertainment services, for example) is up to you. This principle is about saving enough so that you feel comfortable. Put this emergency fund in a separate account from your monthly expenses that you can access within a day or two.

Consider opening a high-yield savings account at a different bank than your normal bank. This will help prevent you from spending your emergency money on non-emergencies. You can earn a higher interest rate on your (untouched) cash.

However, your emergency fund is not there to earn a big return. It's okay if your emergency fund cash sits there without earning much interest. Think of this money as an insurance policy. Insurance policies cost money, but you are glad they are there when you need to use them.

Some personal finance experts recommend saving up to six months of living expenses, but because of the job security in the military, three months should be fine in most circumstances. If you plan to separate soon, a six-to-twelve-month fund may be more appropriate. Set aside enough cash so that you can sleep well at night. That's most important.

Personally, I make sure my emergency fund can cover:

- a $1,000 car repair
- three months of living expenses
- two roundtrip tickets home to see both my family and my wife's family

Even though service members have great job security, the government frequently "shuts down" for political reasons, and military pay is often threatened during these times. Between 2010 to 2020, the federal government shut down three times. Each time, military pay was saved at the last minute, but it was still a concern for many service members.

While it is unlikely that a government shutdown will affect military pay, it is possible. To plan for this, set aside enough cash in an emergency fund, so you can miss a few paychecks and not sweat it. It will give you reassurance through the next government crisis and prevent you from accumulating credit card debt or taking on a personal loan.

PRINCIPLE FIVE:
MAXIMIZE YOUR TAX-ADVANTAGED ACCOUNTS

Contribute the maximum amounts to your individual retirement accounts (IRAs) and employer-sponsored retirement accounts like the TSP. In other personal finance publications, you may read about the "401k plan." This is the civilian version of the TSP.

These accounts have specific tax advantages that allow you to pay less taxes now or less taxes in the future. The government offers these tax breaks to encourage retirement savings and long-term investing.

Retirement accounts come in two flavors: Roth and Traditional. So, you can have a Roth IRA, a Roth TSP, a Traditional IRA, and a Traditional TSP and contribute money to all four accounts each year.

You can mix and match these four types of accounts. Roth accounts are funded with money that's taxed today and Traditional accounts are funded with money that's taxed when you withdraw the money during retirement.

For instance, when you withdraw funds from a Roth retirement account after age 59.5, you do not pay taxes on the contributions you made or any gains those contributions earned. Instead, you pay the taxes this year on the money you contribute today. In other words, Roth accounts are funded with money you have already paid taxes on.

With Traditional retirement accounts, any money you contribute is deducted from that year's taxable income, giving you an immediate tax benefit. These tax savings can be invested today to put you further on your path to FI. In other words, traditional accounts are funded with pre-tax dollars. You don't pay taxes on the money today, but you may have to in the future.

If you are deployed to a combat zone, make sure you maximize both your Roth TSP and Roth IRA. While you're deployed, your pay is tax-free, so you can make tax-free contributions. These tax-free contributions will grow tax-free for many years. When you can withdraw from the accounts after age 59.5, the entire account is tax-free in retirement. This triple tax-free benefit is unique to military members, and I highly encourage you to take full advantage of it.

An excellent initial goal for a young service member is to maximize your TSP and IRA contributions each year. If this seems impossible, work on maximizing your TSP first and then work on your IRA.

You can also contribute to your spouse's IRA if you file taxes jointly, even if your spouse isn't employed. After maxing out TSP and IRA contributions in any given year, continue to save beyond those contribution limits in a taxable investment account which I'll discuss in the section on non-retirement investment accounts. If you can do that in your 20s or 30s, you will be well on your way to early FI.

PRINCIPLE SIX:
SAVINGS RATE BEATS RATE OF RETURN

The most important factor when it comes to achieving rapid FI is your savings rate, not your investment return rate. To determine your savings rate, divide your total annual investments by your total annual income. For example, if you made $60,000 last year after taxes and contributed $6,000 to your Roth IRA, your personal savings rate is 10 percent.

If you hold your investment returns constant, your time until FI is a function of your savings rate. Let's assume a 7 percent investment return, which is close to the S&P 500 index return since 1871. The below graph shows how as your savings rate increases, the amount of time until you reach FI decreases rapidly.

WORKING YEARS TO FINANCIAL INDEPENDENCE

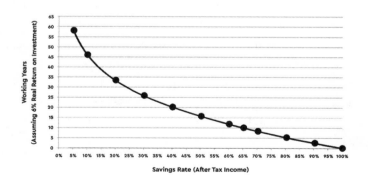

As you can see from the graph, rapid FI is achievable within less than 20 years if you save more than 45 percent of your earnings. Notice that a 10 percent savings rate means you will have to work for 45 years to achieve FI. That's working from age 20 to 65, the standard retirement age. No wonder most personal finance "experts" advocate saving 10 to 15 percent of your income! They are expecting you to work for most of your adult life.

Your savings rate is within your control while your investment returns are mostly out of your control. The market will return what the market returns. Focus on your savings rate.

Achieving an investment return above the average market return is nearly impossible for the average investor. For a good introduction to this topic, read *The Little Book of Common Sense Investing* by Vanguard founder John C. Bogle and *A Random Walk Down Wall Street* by Burton Malkiel.

Even full-time investment professionals who spend years in school, dedicate hours every day studying the markets, and have access to the fastest computers money can buy cannot beat the average index return. The index in this case is usually a large collection of stocks, such as the S&P 500, which includes the largest 500 companies in America. Studies have consistently shown that within various 10-, 15-, and 30-year time periods, over 90 percent of actively managed mutual funds fail to beat their index, after accounting for fees.

As an "average Joe or Jane" investor, your longer-term investment performance will be better by buying passive index funds through TSP or Vanguard compared to trying to pick the best companies or the best fund managers. There is no reliable way to select the 10 percent of actively managed funds that outperform the market in advance; it's only in hindsight that the winners emerge.

Investment returns are mostly out of your control. Savings rate, however, is very much in your control. So, stay focused on your savings rate.

The intelligent military investor focuses on keeping costs low, staying diversified, and achieving the highest savings rate one can reasonably maintain. Rather than trying to outsmart the system, just invest along with the market in index funds and let your savings rate do the heavy lifting.

If you have a passion for stock picking, set aside a small portion of your net worth (5 percent at most) to dabble with carefully. But keep the core of your investments in low-cost, automatic, diversified, and simple (LADS) passive index funds, which we'll address next.

PRINCIPLE SEVEN:
KEEP YOUR INVESTMENTS LADS: LOW-COST, AUTOMATIC, DIVERSIFIED, AND SIMPLE

Of all the investment strategies I've tried, LADS has been my most successful: Low-cost, Automatic, Diversified, and Simple.

Consistent, automatic savings poured into my simple and diversified index funds at low costs have been the cornerstone of my successful investment portfolio. I recommend you do the same.

Even Warren Buffett, famed stock picker and one of the best investors of all time, set a simple, low-cost, S&P 500 index fund as the core of his wife's investment portfolio. We'll address each part of the LADS system in detail in the chapter "Investing While Serving in the Military." For now, just remember to keep your investments LADS!

PRINCIPLE EIGHT:
SPEND MONEY ON WHAT MATTERS MOST TO YOU

Marketing and advertising condition us from an early age to crave and desire things. Kids usually know the McDonald's logo before they can read.

However, when we acquire those things, the happiness associated with the thing quickly fades. This is known as "hedonic adaptation." We quickly become accustomed to new things and then want to move on to the next shiny object.

To maximize your happiness and the happiness of your loved ones, prioritize your spending on the things and experiences that truly bring you pleasure. If you are content with a two-bedroom home, you don't need a three-bedroom home. If you do not care about fancy cars, don't buy a fancy car.

So many of our purchases are simply virtue-, wealth-, or power-signaling to other humans. If you don't play the game of Rolexes, BMWs, and Ford F-150s, you can become wealthier more quickly.

Don't buy things you don't need, with money you don't have, to impress people you don't like.

PRINCIPLE NINE:
BUY INCOME-PRODUCING ASSETS

The rich get richer because they buy income-producing assets like real estate, stocks, bonds, and CDs. When you buy things that do not produce income, you force yourself to continue trading your time as you work for money.

Whenever you want to buy something that costs $1,000, first consider what it would cost to buy an asset that could generate $1,000 of income per year. For instance, a $15,000 investment that returns 7 percent per year yields $1,050 per year. Initially, that asset costs more than the goods you want to buy. But eventually, you'll have the asset, the income from the asset, and the thing you wanted to buy in the first place.

Clearly, you still need to buy things that lose value over time. If you invested all your income into income-producing assets, you would have nothing to eat. But using some of your income to buy income-producing assets is the great mindset shift. Now your money can make money.

This new way of thinking enables you to move away from relying on employment income to fund your lifestyle. By adding additional income sources, you are no longer trading your time for your money. Once your investment income can cover your lifestyle, then you are FI.

ESTABLISHING

YOUR FINANCIAL FOUNDATION

The nine financial principles will serve you well throughout your life regardless of your financial situation. Now let's discuss how to establish your financial foundation. You'll build your fortress of financial independence (FI) on top of this solid foundation.

If you've just joined the military, these tactics will help you build a solid footing. If you've been in the military for a while, you can apply these ideas to your own situation and reclaim your stability.

Topics we'll cover in this chapter are:

- Buying Your First Car
- Housing Choices: On or Off Base, Rent or Buy
- Online Checking and Savings Accounts
- Lifestyle Inflation: Live One Rank Below Your Current Rank
- Budgeting
- Tax Hacking
- Credit Cards, Scores, and Reports
- Debt: Interest Working Against You
- Insurance: Auto, Renters, Home, Life

THE MILITARY MONEY MANUAL

BUYING YOUR FIRST CAR

Joining the military right out of high school or college means you probably don't have much experience buying cars. You may think that now that you're earning a paycheck, you deserve the best car you can get an auto loan for. Don't fall into this trap! Just because you're making a bit of money now doesn't entitle you to a new F-150 or Dodge Charger.

Remember that most of your driving will be to and from work. Commuting will consume about 80 percent of your driving time. Buy a car optimized for that 80 percent.

Your car will also sit there unused for 90 percent of the day. It will sit idle even more if you deploy or go on TDY/TAD orders. If you live on base, especially when you are in training, you may not even need a car since you can get to everywhere you need to go on a bike or by walking.

Yes, cars are convenient and fun. It's important to have a way to get off base and explore. And many bases aren't small enough to support full-time walking. A car is needed at most bases, but you can save a bit of money by not driving for short trips around base. Stay lean, enjoy a good walk or bike ride, and save money.

Remember what Tyler Durden said in the movie *Fight Club*: "You are not the car you drive." You'll see plenty of E-3s driving Ford Mustangs they can't afford while admirals and generals drive 12-year-old champagne-colored Honda Civics. At the end of the day, no one cares what your car looks like, how fast it can go, or how much power your engine has. If you are a car person, then spend your money on a car that brings you joy. For the rest of us non-car people, it's just not important.

A car should safely transport you from Point A to Point B with good gas mileage. If it looks nice, bonus points. Sure, you may get gently mocked by your friends if you drive an older car with some light cosmetic damage, but you can smile knowing you're getting ever closer to FI while they're still paying off the $60,000 Ford F-150 they "got a great deal on" three years ago.

In one fascinating section of the famous wealth-building book *The Millionaire Next Door*, the authors study the types of cars that millionaires drive. They found that more millionaires drive a Honda Civic or a Toyota Camry than a Mercedes Benz or a Lexus. If you want to set yourself up for success, buy used and prioritize reliability. Unless having a luxury car matters a lot to you, luxury cars are for suckers.

Since most of your driving will be commuting back and forth from work and your home, your ideal first car in the military is a five-to-ten-year-old Honda Civic, Toyota Prius, or Mazda3 with 30,000–100,000 miles on it and one previous owner. This kind of car represents the perfect intersection of reliability, comfort, affordability, and economy.

Any reliable car will do, but those are three models that have consistently been highly rated for reliability by consumer groups like *Consumer Reports*. Before buying your first car, look up the latest car reliability reviews at a resource like *Consumer Reports*.

Do not buy a SUV or pickup truck unless you are willing to handicap your journey to FI. The mileage and cost to own one of these vehicles is a massive drag on your finances. And don't fall for the lie that you need to buy a newer or "safer" car once you get married or have kids. Used cars can be safe.

Things to look for in your first car:

- Reliable brand such as Honda, Toyota, or Mazda
- At least 30 MPG (aim for 40+)
- A vehicle that meets 80 percent of your driving needs

Pay cash if you can or get a low-interest-rate loan and pay the loan off as soon as possible. Avoid financing at the dealership, and shop around for a loan before you go car shopping. USAA, Navy Federal, and PenFed typically have great auto loan rates for the military.

Remember that money you spend on a car today is money that you can't invest. The $30,000 you spend on a new car is a depreciating asset. In contrast, if you invest that $30,000, it will grow to $449,000 after 40 years of 7 percent annual return.

If you really enjoy having a nice car, save up until you can afford to pay cash for it. When you have $30,000 sitting in an account, it's quite alarming to see it disappear on just one purchase. You might change your mind and consider investing some of it instead.

HOUSING CHOICES:
ON OR OFF BASE, RENT OR BUY

Living on or off base/post sometimes isn't a choice, but it often can be depending on your rank or family situation. Both on and off base have advantages depending on your base location, family situation, family size, age, and job.

If you live on base you can often walk, run, or bike to work. That can save you thousands of dollars a year in commuting costs. Your spouse might like the community on base, and your kids will likely have many playmates nearby. The proximity of schools, gyms, activities, and commissaries is a great reason to live on base.

When you live on base, government housing will usually take your entire basic allowance for housing (BAH). Depending on your base's location, this may or may not be a good deal.

If you are single or you don't have children, you may enjoy living off base in a lively downtown area or with roommates. If you live off base, you can sometimes find rentals well below your BAH and save the difference. This can mean a substantial ($1,000+/month) increase in your take home income. Note that if you're overseas, you won't be able to pocket your Overseas Housing Allowance (OHA).

Living off base can have many benefits:

- Better schools, parks, and playgrounds
- Better access to downtown areas and activities
- More restaurants, better nightlife, and other entertainment options
- Better quality housing options and more bedrooms
- Closer proximity to your friends or family

If you live off base, you'll have to decide whether to rent or buy. Nine times out of ten, it makes more sense for military families or individual service members to rent their home rather than buy. This is mainly due to the large costs and fees of buying and selling every few years, which is often the amount of time you'll have before relocating.

When renting, you are only responsible for your rent and maybe utilities every month. You can break a rental agreement with 30 days' written notice if you get Permanent Change of Station (PCS), TDY/TAD, or deployment orders for longer than 90 days, thanks again to the Servicemembers Civil Relief Act (SCRA). The flexibility of renting is incredibly useful for the unpredictability of military service.

As a renter, all repairs and maintenance are the responsibility of your landlord. This frees up time for you to do the things you love, rather than doing housework and home repairs. If you enjoy doing housework or yard work, you could ask your landlord if you can do the maintenance yourself and see if they'll reimburse you or reduce your rent.

The true cost of home ownership is never just the mortgage. As a homeowner, you may be responsible for paying principal, interest, property taxes, property insurance, homeowners association (HOA) fees, maintenance, and repairs. Not to mention the transaction costs associated with real estate.

When you buy or sell your home, you will pay realtor fees of around 6 percent, possible sales tax, down payments, and a myriad of other fees on both ends of the transaction. You will also have to invest time and energy into maintaining and repairing your home, unless you want it to decrease in value.

When deciding between buying or renting at your next duty station, keep in mind that most military officers move every three to four years. Enlisted personnel can sometimes remain in place longer, but usually must take PCS orders at some point. You take on tremendous risk by purchasing a home knowing that you will be moving within such a short time frame. If you sell at the end of your assignment, it is unlikely that you will come out ahead except in the luckiest of circumstances.

The break-even point that determines whether someone should rent or buy is usually five to seven years—that's the point at which the transaction costs of buying and selling are finally washed out. This can vary from state to state, but there are plenty of "rent vs. buy" calculators available if you do a quick search online.

If you decide to buy, you can rent your property out when you leave. But this means you will always have to make those mortgage payments, whether you have a renter or not. Have you thought about how you will pay the mortgage on your property if it's vacant for three months? The cost of an empty rental property can add up quickly.

The stress levels associated with being a long-distance landlord are not trivial. Even if you have a property manager, friend, or family member look after the rental property, no one will look after your investment better than you can and having a property manager will reduce your potential earnings. All it takes is one AC repair bill or a leaking roof to destroy months of "earnings" on your rental property.

Don't think of your rent as "throwing money away every month." You are paying your landlord for a place to live, and they are accepting the risk of home ownership. It is the property owner's capital that is tied up in the house. Meanwhile, you get to live in the property, and at the end of your assignment, you can move without the hassle of having to sell or rent it out.

With all those negative factors, you might think no one buys. However, many service members own property around the world. Some even make positive cash flow on their properties and enjoy being long-distance landlords. Many military real estate investors take advantage of the VA Loan, a special mortgage offered to veterans by the US Department of Veterans Affairs. This is a loan offered by private organizations but guaranteed by the VA, so the interest rates, closing costs, and required down payments are often much lower than civilian mortgages. Even with advantages like the VA Loan, long-distance landlording and property investment is not for everyone. Don't assume it's for you, especially early in your career.

Do your research and leave yourself an exit strategy. There are many anecdotes about military families successfully buying properties at each duty station and renting them when they leave, but there are even more stories of families who bought homes and regretted the decision. Please do exhaustive research before any real estate purchase.

If you do buy, do not bite off more than you can chew. Overspending on a home is one of the fastest ways to get yourself in trouble financially. As a rule of thumb, I recommend spending no more than two-thirds of your BAH per month on mortgage, taxes, HOA dues, and insurance.

This rule of thumb should keep you out of trouble in case you receive late-notice PCS orders. This happened to many military homeowners between 2008 and 2014. On the heels of the recession, they could not sell their property for a gain, nor could they find renters quickly. You never know when the next housing market collapse, recession, or pandemic will happen.

Remember that your BAH will go up and down as you move. So be careful buying near your BAH limit for your current duty station. And just because the Department of Defense gives you thousands for housing every month does not mean you need to spend all of it. Feel free to pocket the difference between your housing expenses and this tax-free housing allowance. It's an easy way to accelerate your journey towards FI.

Housing is often the most expensive part of a service member's budget. If you're single, one idea to reduce costs is to get a roommate. It could cut your expenses in half or allow you to live in a nicer apartment or better area of town. It also gives you a built-in social network, which can be important if many members of your unit have kids or are already married.

I've tried several ways of solving the housing problem. I've lived on base in government housing, rented off base, and lived off base in a condo I purchased. Having experienced all these options, I am an advocate for renting either on or off base while on active duty. The flexibility to PCS quickly, without the stress of long-distance landlording or selling your property, is priceless.

ONLINE CHECKING AND SAVING ACCOUNTS

Your future FI is based on two fundamental accounts: a checking account for spending and a savings account for short-term savings. Both accounts need to be at an FDIC-insured bank or credit union.

Checking accounts are designed for unlimited monthly transactions and usually pay less interest than a savings account. Checking accounts have a debit card connected to them so you can make purchases anywhere debit cards are accepted or withdraw cash from an ATM.

A checking account is good for paying bills, buying everyday essentials, and getting cash. Make sure that whatever bank you use offers free ATM withdrawals and reimburses you if you are charged a withdrawal fee. Search online for "banks with no ATM fees."

Savings accounts usually pay slightly higher interest rates than checking accounts. These accounts are good for saving for infrequent expenses, long- or short-term goals, or emergency funds.

There are also accounts marketed as high-yield savings accounts or HYSAs. These are usually online, FDIC insured accounts that pay 10x or even 100x the average interest rate. Search "high-yield savings accounts" and you should have dozens of options to choose from. Read reviews from other users online to make sure the bank is reputable and doesn't play any games with your money.

Besides a checking and savings account, I recommend opening an account or sub-account for each goal you are saving for. It's okay to have dozens of savings accounts and checking accounts all at the same bank. By having multiple accounts, you can more easily separate money into different buckets to save for goals. For instance, here's how I use my four checking accounts:

- The first receives my military paycheck and automatically transfers my money into my other accounts on the 1st and 15th of the month. Whatever is leftover in this account is my money to live on until the next paycheck.

- Another account is for paying my bills. Any time I make a credit card purchase, I put the amount of the purchase into this account, withdrawing from whatever savings or checking account is most appropriate. I pay my credit cards in full every month. I also send my rent or mortgage payment electronically from this account. This is an outgoing-transfer-only account.

- One checking account is in my name and one checking account is in my wife's name. These two accounts hold our separate money that we can each spend however we want. That way we can combine our finances to save for the big goals but also keep some separate money for our personal spending.

I recommend having multiple savings accounts. Here's a few ideas of accounts I've had to save for specific goals:

- An emergency fund with three months of expenses

- Holiday and birthday gifts

- Auto repair, insurance, and utilities

- Charity fund to donate at the end of the year

- Travel and vacation fund

Break up your money into separate buckets like this to make it easier to track. It's too difficult to keep track of the money if it's all mixed together in one account.

Keep separate accounts for each goal or expense you're saving for. You can usually add nicknames to the accounts, so you remember exactly what they're for. When you have sub-accounts, it'll be much harder to accidentally spend your Christmas present money on your 4th of July family vacation.

Some banks I recommend are USAA, Navy Federal Credit Union (NFCU), Pentagon Federal Credit Union (PenFed), Ally Bank, or any bank or credit union that is online, does not charge fees for any normal services, and refunds your ATM fees.

The bank should offer no fees on minimum balances in your accounts, no overdraft fees, free overdraft protection, no minimum usage fees, and no account maintenance fees, to name a few.

If a bank ever charges you a fee, consider leaving them immediately and finding one that will not charge you a fee for routine usage. I haven't paid a single banking fee in over 10 years and neither should you.

LIFESTYLE INFLATION: LIVE AT LEAST ONE RANK BELOW YOUR CURRENT RANK

If you're not deliberate with your money, your spending will adjust to your income level. Why do you think millionaire athletes go broke? It's because they spend more as their income goes up. This phenomenon is also known as "lifestyle creep" or "lifestyle inflation."

As you make more money, your habits change. You eat out more, you buy more toys, you buy a boat, you drive a nicer car, you live in a larger house, and you take more vacations.

If you can avoid lifestyle creep for just the first two years after you join the military, you will set yourself up for financial success incredibly early in your life.

To avoid lifestyle creep, live at least one rank below your current rank.

If you are an E-5, live like an E-4. When you get a promotion, increase your TSP contribution a few percentage points. Your pay will go up and so will your savings rate.

While you are a second lieutenant (O-1), live like a cadet. When you pin on captain (O-3), live like a first lieutenant (O-2). Never live a pay grade above your current rank. That's how you get into trouble with debt and living beyond your means.

Spend money on things and experiences that matter to you. Don't worry about what anyone else or "society" thinks.

Keep your expenses low on the big three life expenses: housing, transportation, and food. Then you should have money left over for the things that bring you the most joy.

BUDGETING

When you are on the road to FI, you should know where your money is going. Budgeting gives you a plan and guardrails to keep you from straying too far from the path to wealth.

There are many good apps and websites out there to help you track your spending. Mint, Personal Capital, and You Need a Budget (YNAB) are all easy to set up and easy to use.

My recommended budget is the "anti-budget." Instead of taking the time to track every category and every last dollar, I prefer to set an aggressive savings goal and then not worry about the rest. If I'm saving 50 percent of my take home pay, why does it matter if I spent a little extra on groceries last month?

If you need to know where to start and want to do a more detailed budget, simply write down all your monthly expenses. Identifying where your money is going helps you recognize whether or not your spending is in line with your personal goals.

Some will understand why they're having a hard time paying their rent each month if they just list all the monthly entertainment, streaming, music, and shopping subscriptions.

It adds up quickly if you're not aware of where your money is going.

Setting an automatic monthly savings target and then giving yourself the freedom to spend whatever is left in your checking account removes guilt, stress, and makes it much easier to meet your savings goals.

How much of your pay should you invest? It's up to you, but I recommend saving 50 percent if you want to rapidly achieve FI. If you can beat that goal, awesome—you will get to FI that much faster. Even at 25 percent, you'll set yourself up for FI in less than 35 years.

With a solid spending plan or budget, every month you get to decide what you do with thousands of dollars.

You can choose to spend all of your paycheck now, thus deciding to work for the rest of your life. Or you can invest a significant amount of your income and reduce your required working years by decades.

The great thing about FI is its flexibility. You choose when you achieve it and at what level you finish. You decide what is best for your situation and goals.

TAX HACKING

One way to increase your monthly take-home pay is to establish residency in one of the income tax-free states. Laws change, but in 2021, those states are Alaska, Florida, Nevada, New Hampshire, Tennessee, Texas, Washington, and Wyoming. If you are lucky enough to be stationed in one of these states, consider switching your tax residency to this state. You can still vote in your home state and maintain a "home of record" in your home state.

All it takes to establish tax residency is filling out a few simple forms with your military finance section.

Establishing residency is easy to do if you are stationed in that state. If you are not stationed in one of these income tax-free states it may be trickier, but it's still worth looking into. Some states also have special laws that do not allow the taxation of military pay.

Talk to your finance office about your options. Not paying state income taxes could save you hundreds of dollars every month.

If you've just joined the military, I recommend taking the time to do your own tax return. Tax forms are usually released by the end of January each year. Sometimes you'll need to wait until the end of February for corrected forms.

If you only have military income to report from your W-2 tax form, the tax return will be very simple. Additionally, most online tax providers do military returns for free. Military OneSource, a service members' support agency of the Department of Defense, offers free tax software every year.

You answer a few questions, type in a few numbers from your tax documents, and you can be done in less than an hour. Free tax counselors on base/post or over the phone are also available during tax season.

As a service member, your taxes will be very low relative to your income. If you are receiving BAH and basic allowance for subsistence (BAS), know that these are untaxed allowances. Depending on where you're deployed, your military income may be entirely tax-free thanks to Combat Zone Tax Exclusion (CZTE) pay.

Because of these tax breaks, your taxable income would be much higher in the civilian world. Take advantage of these tax breaks by using Roth accounts and stuffing your retirement accounts full of untaxed income while you serve.

File your tax return on time every year. April 15th is usually the due date. Don't be late! But if you're still waiting on documents, need a corrected W-2, or are busy on a deployment, you can file for an extension until October with a single one-page form available on the IRS website.

CREDIT CARDS, SCORES, AND REPORTS

The path to "good credit" is simple: Apply for just one cash-back rewards card, put your grocery and gas purchases on it, and pay it off online at least once a month. Rinse and repeat for the next five to seven years, and you will have a credit score better than 90 percent of the population.

You may want to start with a card from one of the military banks, like USAA or Navy Federal. They are usually more willing than non-military banks to give you a card with the following important features:

- No annual fees
- At least 1 percent cash back or rewards points
- Bonus rewards of 2+ percent
- A Visa or Mastercard, because American Express and Discover don't have the same global acceptance

That said, of the dozens of credit cards out there, most offer annual fee waivers for US military members and their spouses. If you'd like to learn more about fee-waived credit cards for military personnel, I offer a free online course at militarymoneymanual.com/umc3.

Personally, I use a cash-back card, travel rewards card, and others as my everyday cards. Once you've established good credit, you can take advantage of cards with waived annual fees for military members.

When selecting a card, I look for travel reward credit cards with military waived annual fees, welcome spending bonuses worth thousands of dollars, and spending bonus categories like restaurants, groceries, gas, hotels, and airfare.

Some credit card companies offer SCRA or MLA benefits to their military cardholders. To refresh, the SCRA, or Servicemembers Civil Relief Act, protects service members from certain civil and legal penalties while serving on active duty and applies to accounts opened before their active-duty service began. MLA stands for Military Lending Act and applies to credit or loan accounts opened after active-duty service starts.

Each company interprets the details of the SCRA and MLA a little differently. American Express and Chase, for instance, do not charge military service members annual fees on any of their personal cards, including high-end, $500+ per year travel cards like Chase Sapphire Reserve or American Express Platinum. This allows you to get these cards, along with their great welcome bonuses and annual perks, for free.

For instance, some of the high-end travel cards have annual travel credits for $300. That means you can get $300 worth of airfare for free every year, without paying the annual fee. It sounds too good to be true, but I have personally benefited from SCRA and MLA deals for over a decade.

I urge you to do your research on SCRA and MLA benefits for the best credit cards. Some service members who use these cards have received hundreds or even thousands of dollars in reimbursements of fees and interest charges. But only take advantage of these benefits if you're in a good spot financially and responsible enough to pay your bill each month. Never carry a balance.

Credit cards are the easiest, cheapest, and best way to build a credit score. If you want to buy a home with a mortgage, travel hack, or get the best credit cards available, then you should work on building an excellent credit score. Having a good credit score will save you thousands of dollars a year by allowing you to qualify for lower interest rates.

A good credit score is key to being eligible for the best cash-back or travel rewards cards. These cards are only available to those with excellent credit. These cards offer perks that you can't get with basic cards, like airport lounge access, free hotel room upgrades, no checked baggage fees, no foreign transaction fees, and discounted airfare through their rewards programs.

Credit scores are available for free through several websites. Never pay to obtain your credit score or for "credit score monitoring." These are recurring monthly services that offer little for how much they cost. There are many companies that offer free credit scores and free credit monitoring. They make their money by advertising credit cards or other financial products you may be eligible for.

I recommend CreditKarma.com or CreditSesame.com if you want to obtain your score. Chase, USAA, American Express, and many other banks and credit cards also offer free credit scores and credit monitoring to their customers. It's worth repeating: you should never pay to access your credit score.

Credit reports get pulled any time you want to access more credit, whether to buy a house with a mortgage, buy a car with an auto loan, or get a new credit card. These reports are compiled by the three credit bureaus in the US: TransUnion, Experian, and Equifax.

You are eligible, under federal law, to receive your credit report from each company once per year for free at annualcreditreport.com. This is the only official site for obtaining your federally mandated, free annual credit report.

I recommend setting a reminder in your calendar to pull one report every four months from one of the credit bureaus, and rotate which bureau you use each time. This gives you the best chance of catching any error or fraudulent activity.

Once you have a firm grasp of how to use credit cards, you may be interested in travel hacking. Travel hacking is a system where you use credit card welcome bonuses to earn miles and points that you can redeem for cash, hotel stays, or air travel. You can even redeem these credit card points for business or first-class flying experiences or five-star hotel rooms that would ordinarily cost many thousands of dollars. I cover travel hacking in a later chapter in this book.

DEBT: INTEREST WORKING AGAINST YOU

Debt can be a good thing. Debt is what allows people to start businesses and to purchase expensive equipment to increase their productivity. Debt, through a mortgage, allows Americans to buy homes worth many times their annual salaries. This is what people mean by "smart" debt.

Smart debt is usually backed by an appreciating asset. For instance, a mortgage has a real property behind it, student loans can increase your earning potential with a degree, and a business loan can help you acquire material to start or expand your business.

Despite these positive uses, debt is usually a negative for the average American. Personal loans, payday loans, and credit card debt are all examples of consumer debt that are compounding interest to make you poorer, not richer. It's the opposite of investing. Rather than your money working for you, you are working for your money. You do not get to decide what happens to each dollar you receive until your debt is paid off. This is "dumb" debt.

For officers, one common military loan is the cadet loan, midshipman loan, or commissioning loan, offered by a few military-friendly banks. This loan is usually offered a year prior to your commissioning and for a year afterwards.

Some smart uses for this low-interest loan are paying off higher-interest debt like student loans, buying a reliable car to get you started in your military career, investing in your IRAs, or helping you make first month's rent at your first duty station. The cadet loan is an excellent way to start your military career if you need it.

Do not accumulate dumb debt. If it's not a mortgage, you probably don't need it. Avoid debt like the plague, and you will end up far ahead of your peers and fellow military investors.

INSURANCE: AUTO, RENTERS, HOME, LIFE

Insurance is risk management. You pay a bank or insurance company a few dollars to ensure that if something catastrophic happens to your car, your stuff, your home, or yourself, you are not financially ruined.

As a young military service member, your insurance needs are pretty basic. Auto, home or renters, and term life insurance are all you really need. Health insurance will be covered for you and your family for free under Tricare.

Auto insurance is a must and usually required by state law. Do not be afraid to shop around. Compare quotes from all the main insurance companies like USAA, GEICO, and others. Make sure to ask for a military discount.

If you deploy, store your car and call your insurance company to reduce your monthly payments. Rates are usually cheap for a car in storage.

If you only take on as much auto insurance as you need, you can save hundreds every year. If you drive an older, used car—like the one you should be buying—you can forgo the comprehensive and collision coverage. This should save you several hundred dollars per year and you can insure yourself against a totaled car with your emergency fund.

Renters insurance is cheap (usually less than $50 per month) and will cover you if the unlikely happens. If you buy property, get good homeowners' insurance. Make sure that you are covered for whatever disaster tends to plague your region, such as hurricanes, flooding, tornadoes, earthquakes, or volcanoes.

Servicemembers Group Life Insurance (SGLI) and Family Servicemembers Group Life Insurance (FSGLI) are cheap and convenient term life insurance. It only costs about a dollar a day for full coverage, up to $400,000.

If you die while on active-duty orders, your beneficiary, the person you appoint to receive your insurance payment, will also receive a "death gratuity" from the government of $100,000. Five hundred thousand dollars' worth of insurance should be plenty for a young, unmarried service member.

If your family grows, you may want additional term life insurance coverage. If you are married and have kids or other dependents, you can acquire additional life insurance beyond SGLI. There are many cheap options for adding additional coverage through American Armed Forces Mutual Aid Association (AAFMAA), Navy Mutual Life Insurance, USAA, and others. Be sure to pick a policy that covers military-related or war-related death.

SGLI is convenient as it comes right out of your paycheck. It covers you at home and at war. If you suffer an early death, you do not want to leave a legacy of debt or financial hardship for your loved ones.

Pay the monthly premium and get the full $400,000 of coverage. The monthly premium is even reimbursed if you are in a combat zone. That's free insurance when you need it most. If you're married, get a quote for term life insurance from a military-friendly insurer or use the FSGLI.

Do not use whole life insurance or any product that bundles investing with your life insurance. You will be much better off if you purchase term life insurance and invest in separate accounts like IRAs or the TSP.

Whole life insurance plans are expensive products that do little to benefit you and instead offer generous commissions to those who sell them. A few financial companies are notorious for selling unnecessary insurance and investment products to military service members. Stay away from them. Stick with term life insurance if you need it.

INVESTING WHILE SERVING
IN THE MILITARY

We've established the foundation for financial success.

You should now have:

- A reliable and inexpensive car

- Smart housing choices

- A system of bank accounts for automatically transferring money to investment and savings accounts

- An awareness of lifestyle inflation and how to avoid it

- A budget that allows you to pay your bills, have fun, and invest a large percentage of your paycheck

- A smart state tax strategy

- One or two credit cards that you pay off every month

- A commitment to no more debt accumulation

- Insurance to cover yourself

With this foundation established, we'll now get to the core subject of this book: how to invest to achieve financial independence (FI) in the military. Here's how to do it, in less than 100 words:

Keep your investments low-cost, automatic, diversified and simple (LADS). Maximize your tax-advantaged investment accounts. Start with the Roth TSP, then open a Vanguard account for your Roth IRA.

If you do not have the desire or willingness to learn how to create your own asset allocation, just invest in the TSP Lifecycle Fund that matches your retirement age and a Vanguard Target Retirement Fund. Keep the majority (95+ percent) of your assets in low-cost index funds. Invest monthly via automatic transfer. Let compounding do the rest.

WHY BOTHER INVESTING?

Let's start with a discussion on why we invest. We invest so that our money will grow, hopefully faster than inflation, to a point where we can live off our investments.

If invested wisely, our money can work harder and make us more money than we ever could. Every dollar is a little employee that you can put to work. Given enough time, these little employees can generate more income per year than you can.

Investing is putting our savings into income-producing assets or assets that grow in value, also known as appreciating assets. At the end of each decade, your net worth should increase, rather than decrease. Investing is what separates the rich from the poor. When you invest, you take control of your financial situation and future. Small investments, compounded over time, yield amazing results that enable your financial freedom.

Most people lack the time, energy, or knowledge to invest. I hope that this chapter can resolve those issues for you and allow you to join the investing class. After all, why should they be the only ones to get ahead?

So, what can we invest in? Examples of assets include:

- real estate, such as houses, property, land, and buildings

- businesses, usually through stocks (shares of the company)

- savings accounts

- certificates of deposit (CDs)

- gold or other precious metals

- bonds (loans to governments or corporations)

- an ownership stake in a small business

A good investment grows in value or produces income, beats inflation, and rewards you properly for the risks you take.

Why do you have to beat inflation? Inflation is the insidious little monster chasing savers. It constantly gnaws at your savings, decreasing their value. It's why you can't just stick your money in a mattress for 30 years.

Which investments beat inflation? To give you an idea, here's some data on the performance of various investments from 1802 to 2001, taken from the book *Stocks for the Long Run*. The average annual returns in this chart are "real," or after inflation. So if your asset grew at the same rate as inflation, the average real rate of return would be 0 percent.

Asset Class	Current Value of $1 Invested in 1802	Average Annual Real Rate of Return
Stocks	$802,326	6.6%
Bonds	$1,552	3.5%
Treasury Bills	$281	2.7%
Gold	$3.44	0.6%
Dollar	$0.052	-1.4%

As you can see from the chart, gold barely beats inflation. If you just keep dollars in your mattress, they are worth 1.4% less every year.

Stocks, bonds, and real estate are the only consistent long-term wealth-generating tools available to you. The US stock market has returned an average of 6 to 7 percent per year since the 1870s, after inflation. It's the greatest wealth generating tool in the world.

Next you may be wondering: how do I invest in these things? How do I buy appreciating, income-producing assets and grow my net worth?

THE THRIFT SAVINGS PLAN EXPLAINED

Your most essential investment account while serving in the military is the Thrift Savings Plan or TSP. The TSP allows you to invest in appreciating, income-producing assets and grow your net worth.

If you have ever heard of a "401k," this is the military's version. It's an employer-sponsored retirement plan as opposed to an IRA, which is an individual retirement account.

An employer-sponsored plan just means your employer does some of the paperwork to get the account started. You will still need to start your contributions and set up your account access on TSP.gov.

The TSP is one of the most underutilized military benefits. Consistent investment in your TSP is an easy road to FI. Here's what you need to do to start investing in your TSP:

1. Login to your military pay site (usually myPay) and set up TSP contributions. Make sure your physical address is correct as the TSP mails your initial password to you.

2. Log in to TSP.gov and create an account.

3. Set up a "contribution allocation" on TSP.gov. This is the investing plan for each contribution you automatically send to the TSP from your paycheck.

4. If you already have money in the TSP, make sure it is invested how you want it to be. You can do an "interfund transfer" to move any money you already have in the TSP to a different fund.

The TSP is a retirement account that you fund with your military paycheck. You set the percentage of your pay that you want to contribute to the TSP on the myPay website or wherever you manage your military paycheck. The money will automatically deposit into your TSP account and be invested in accordance with the contribution allocation plan you established on the TSP.gov website.

If you are part of the Blended Retirement System, or BRS, as every new military recruit has been since 2018, then you can receive a 5 percent matching contribution. It doesn't matter whether you contribute to the Roth TSP or Traditional TSP: the 5 percent match goes into your Traditional TSP, due to tax reasons. Note that the 5 percent match does not count against your annual elective deferral limit, which in 2021, is $19,500.

The BRS match is a fantastic benefit of the military retirement system. The match can be worth tens of thousands of dollars over your lifetime.

Once you set up your contribution on myPay, next you need to log in to TSP.gov and make sure your contribution allocation is correct. This is the plan for every dollar you contribute to the TSP.

This is where you get to pick your asset allocation and decide the percentage of portfolio in US stocks, international stocks, and bonds. Don't know which fund to contribute to? Let's review the TSP funds.

The TSP is broken into five main funds:

- **C Fund**: Common Stock Index. The 500 largest companies in America, also known as the S&P 500.

- **S Fund**: Small Cap Stock Index. The other 3,000+ publicly traded companies in America. With the C and the S Fund, you can own every publicly traded company in America.

- **I Fund**: International Stock Index. Own 900 companies outside the United States in countries like Japan, United Kingdom, France, and Australia.

- **F Fund**: Fixed Income Index. Total US bond market, where you are loaning money to governments and companies.

- **G Fund**: Government Securities. Backed by the US government, the least volatile fund and the lowest long-run returns.

If you don't know where to begin with these five funds, the Lifecycle Funds are perfect for you. Lifecycle Funds are built from the five main funds. These are expertly designed funds that provide you with the best expected returns for the risk appropriate for you.

When you're young, the Lifecycle Funds are 99 percent stocks and one percent bonds. More stocks mean more volatility (prices go up and down quickly) but also a better chance for higher long-run returns.

As you get older, the Lifecycle Fund automatically rebalances and becomes more stable but with lower expected returns. As you near retirement age, the Lifecycle Fund tilts to 70 percent bonds and 30 percent stocks, flipping the ratio it kept when you were young.

We'll talk about why I recommend Lifecycle Funds for most military investors later in this chapter.

WHERE TO START INVESTING: ROTH TSP AND ROTH IRAS

The easiest option to begin investing in stocks and bonds is with retirement accounts. In the military, you can have both IRA and TSP accounts and contribute the maximum amount allowed to both.

These accounts reduce your taxes, letting you keep more of your money. We discussed in a previous chapter that retirement accounts like the TSP and IRA come in two different flavors: Traditional and Roth.

Traditional accounts are not taxed today, but you will most likely pay taxes when you withdraw the money in retirement. These are good for high-income earners and perhaps later in your career.

The other flavor of IRAs and TSPs are Roth accounts, named for Senator William Roth of Delaware. In these accounts, you pay taxes when you contribute but not when you withdraw the money. These are better for young military service members trying to build wealth because much of your pay is tax-free.

There are two accounts inside your TSP: a traditional TSP and a Roth TSP. You can contribute to one or both TSPs in one calendar year. The contribution limit for the TSP changes every year or two, but in 2021, the limit is $19,500. That's $19,500 total between the traditional and Roth TSP accounts.

The other retirement account options are traditional or Roth IRAs; you can have one or both types of accounts. These accounts share the same annual contribution limit. You can mix and match contributions, so long as you don't exceed the annual limit. For example, the maximum IRA contribution in 2021 is $6,000. That limit applies to all your IRA accounts, both Traditional and Roth.

You can contribute the full amount to either a Roth or Traditional IRA, or you can contribute to both. For example, you could put $3,000 in a Roth IRA and $3,000 in a Traditional IRA. But you're allowed to make any combination as long as the total doesn't exceed the annual contribution limit.

The IRA contribution limit is separate from and does not affect your TSP contribution limit. In other words, you can contribute the maximum amount to both your IRA and TSP. In 2021, that's $6,000 + $19,500 = $25,500 per year of total contributions to your Roth IRA and Roth TSP. These IRA annual contribution limits are published by the IRS each year and can increase (but never decrease), just like the TSP contribution limit.

For IRAs, you must open the account yourself. Most IRAs can be created in less than 10 minutes. You can hold your IRA at thousands of financial institutions. Schwab, Fidelity, and Vanguard are some of the most popular IRA accounts. I recommend Vanguard for your IRAs.

It's important to prioritize your investment into retirement accounts for three reasons:

1. Money invested in a Roth account can grow untaxed for the rest of your working life and be withdrawn untaxed in retirement.

2. Your taxes can be immediately reduced by contributing to a Traditional retirement plan, and you can grow those tax savings.

3. The retirement account option available to military service members, the TSP, is one of the best in the world when it comes to cost, simplicity, and diversification.

In summary: we invest to grow our assets and to eventually become FI. Stocks and corporate or government bonds are the most consistent long-term growth assets. We prioritize funding our retirement accounts because of their tax advantages.

Your investments should be a simple mix of US stocks, international stocks, and bond index funds that track the entire global market passively.

Now let's talk about how to select investments. As discussed earlier in the book, my number-one investing principle is to follow the LADS system: low-cost, automatic, diversified, and simple.

LADS: LOW-COST

Action: Select low-cost index funds with low-cost expense ratios. All of the funds in the TSP meet these criteria and many Vanguard funds do as well.

Background: Unlike most things in life, when it comes to investing, the less you pay, the better your result. Studies like the SPIVA scorecard, published by the S&P Dow Jones Indices, definitively show that your portfolio performance will be better over the long run with low-cost passive index funds rather than more expensive, actively managed funds.

You don't need to pay high fees for an actively managed mutual fund that has no guarantee of outperforming the basic index fund. Low-cost funds have consistently beaten actively managed funds over 5-, 10-, 15-, and 30-year time periods. So stick with low-cost TSP and Vanguard funds.

Expense ratios are calculated by how much of your assets the fund manager takes annually to pay the expenses of the fund. Fund managers' salaries, bonuses, computers, and marketing are all costs that go into the expense ratio.

For the TSP, the expense ratio is usually less than 0.05 percent. That means for every $1,000 you invest, you pay only 50 cents a year. A million-dollar TSP portfolio would only cost $500 per year to manage. The rest of the return (or loss) of your invested assets goes to you. Low-cost is one reason the TSP is such a great deal for military and government employees. When you leave the military, you can choose to keep your TSP open and let it continue to grow with all the low-cost benefits included.

Vanguard, Schwab, and Fidelity all have total market index funds that charge comparable costs to the TSP. Vanguard's corporate structure makes the owners of the index fund shares the owners of the company, so Vanguard is not as profit-seeking as other investment firms. For this reason, I recommend Vanguard for your investments beyond the TSP.

Cost is the most important factor in determining your investment returns. If you are paying a 1 percent expense ratio, you must make at least a 1 percent return just to break even. The difference between paying 1 percent and 0.05 percent on your investments adds up substantially over time. For comparison, the average mutual fund may charge 1 percent and the TSP and Vanguard funds are usually around 0.05 percent or less.

Over 40 years—the average investing lifetime—someone who pays 1 percent expense ratios will lose 33 percent of their total returns to fees. That means a $10,000 investment growing at 7 percent per year for 40 years will only be worth $103,000, whereas it would have been worth $147,000 if you had paid the lower annual fee. See the chart below for the effect of paying 0.05 percent versus 1 percent in expense ratio fees.

PAY .05% VS PAY 1% FEES

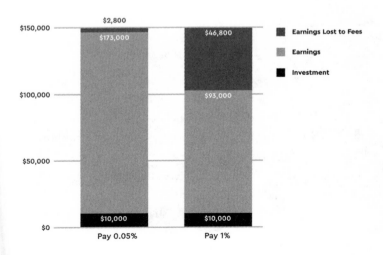

81

Keeping your investment expenses low is something you can control, unlike the performance of the investment, which is completely out of your control. Focus on the investment factors you can control such as cost, diversity, automatic diversification, and savings rate. Let the market provide the return that it will. With inflation also dragging you down, any fund with a cost above 0.30 percent is too much of a drag on your gains.

With low-cost index funds, you pay pennies for your investments, allowing you to keep more of your returns. Read the books *A Random Walk Down Wall Street* and *The Little Book of Common Sense Investing* for the in-depth math behind why index funds will always outperform actively managed funds in the long run.

As Warren Buffett said: "Performance comes, performance goes. Fees never falter." Focus on minimizing your fees to maximize your gains.

LADS: AUTOMATIC

Action: Set up automatic contributions from your military paycheck to your TSP. Then, set up automatic withdrawals from your checking account to your IRA. Invest monthly or after every paycheck. If you receive a lump sum payment, like a bonus, invest it as soon as possible.

Background: Automatically investing every paycheck or on a monthly schedule takes emotions and market timing out of the equation. Yes, you will buy high sometimes. Yes, you will buy low sometimes. But in the long run, you will buy through both good and bad times. The important thing is time *in* the market, not timing the market.

Make your investments as automatic as possible. Take decision-making and emotions out of the process of selecting your next investment. For the TSP, set up automatic contributions through myPay, Marine OnLine, or DirectAccess. Contribute as much as you can monthly, up to the annual limit, so you receive the 5 percent match every month, if you're in the BRS.

Decision fatigue is a real thing. You only have a certain amount of willpower to make decisions throughout the day. If you can make a choice that eliminates 100 other choices, you save that willpower for something else important. Automation allows you to make a choice once and reap the benefits from that choice for years. Set up automatic contributions to your TSP once, and you won't have to worry about it again for months or years.

You won't even notice the money is gone from your paycheck if it never reaches your bank account. You'll also never have to worry if you're buying high or buying low. You won't have the agony of buying on February 19, 2020, and watching your investment get cut almost in half in the next 30 days due to the Coronavirus market crash.

By investing automatically every month, you simply buy at whatever price the market sets that particular day. Some days your purchase will be a good deal, while other days it will be overpriced, but over the long run you will put your money to work quickly and without any stress of trying to time the market.

For your IRAs, set up automatic contributions once a month or twice a month on the 1st and 15th, so that you reach the maximum annual limit by the end of the year or as quickly as you can afford. I like to front-load my IRAs and fund them quickly at the start of the year, usually in the first week of January. Select a simple asset allocation and stick with it.

Here are some additional tips to get you started:

- Start out with a 5 percent automated contribution to your TSP through myPay so you earn your full BRS match. I recommended contributing to your Roth TSP first. Do that right now. Do it with your first military paycheck.

- Prioritize your TSP and IRA, your tax-advantaged investment accounts.

- Go with the Roth option if you deploy, are enlisted, or are below O-4. Or lower your taxable income today by contributing to your traditional TSP.

- Develop an asset-allocation plan or personal investing policy statement. Write an email to yourself, your spouse, or keep it with your important documents. Stick with your plan through good markets and bad. Know the math and historical data behind your plan so you can stay the course.

- If you are in the BRS, don't max out your TSP account before December every year. The 5 percent BRS match is paid monthly, so you need to contribute at least 5 percent every month to earn your full matching for the year.

LADS: DIVERSIFIED

Action: Don't buy one company's stock. Buy stocks from many companies with index funds.

Background: One of the best things about buying index funds is that you get automatic diversification. For instance, the Vanguard Total Stock Market Fund (VTSAX), the gold standard in index funds, owns shares in over 3,000 American companies. Buy one fund and you are instantly an owner of 3,000 publicly traded companies in America.

Diversification means not concentrating too much of your wealth in any one company or asset. A single company can easily go bankrupt. But it's unlikely that the entire American economy will go bankrupt. See the resiliency of the American and world economy in the Global Financial Crisis of 2008 and the COVID-19 pandemic of 2020.

You can achieve diversification through a reasonable mixture of US stocks, international stocks, and bonds. This is called your "asset allocation." The easiest way to do this in the military's TSP is to buy the Lifecycle Funds. Pick the fund that is closest to your retirement age. If you turn 60 in 2065, pick the Lifecycle 2065 fund.

US stocks can be bought with funds like VTSAX or the TSP C Fund and S Fund. International stocks are acquired through the Vanguard Total International Stock Market Fund (VTIAX) or the I Fund in TSP. Corporate and government bonds can be purchased with Vanguard Total Bond Fund (VBMFX) or the TSP F Fund and G Fund.

By investing in diversified assets, you earn the double benefit of higher returns with less risk.

Never put all your eggs in one basket. Instead, buy all the eggs and all the baskets. Don't look for a needle in a haystack, either— identifying the next Microsoft, Apple, or Google is next to impossible. Instead, buy the whole haystack and you will have some of the needles inside it.

Time and again you will hear of employees whose entire retirement portfolio was invested in the company they work for. Unfortunately for them, the companies were Enron (filed for bankruptcy in 2001) or Lehman Brothers (collapsed in 2008). And there are others. By not diversifying, you are betting your life savings on the survival of a single company. Rather than risk losing your fortune because of the failure of a single company, spread your risk around. Invest in every company that is publicly available. When you purchase index funds as described above, you are nearly eliminating your risk of complete loss.

You can own shares in every single publicly traded company in America and most publicly traded foreign companies. If all of them go bankrupt or fail, we will have bigger problems to deal with than the collapse of your retirement savings.

When you invest in the TSP and broadly diversified stock and bond funds, you gain automatic diversification. You can own a piece of the 3,000 publicly traded companies in the US for less cost than owning one share of a big company.

That's why there's no better or simpler diversification strategy than investing in total stock and bond market index funds.

LADS: SIMPLE

Action: Never invest in anything you don't understand. If you can't explain it to a five-year-old, it's too complicated. Avoid options trading, shady real estate deals, commodities like gold, oil, and cryptocurrencies like Bitcoin. Buy income-producing assets like stocks, bonds, and real estate.

Background: If you've applied the three previous principles of the LADS system, you'll now have a low-cost, automated, and diversified investment portfolio. The final criterion for successful investing is to keep it simple.

You can achieve excellent returns, global diversification, keep costs low, and automatically grow your net worth with a simple Three-Fund Portfolio that includes a:

- **total US stock market fund**. At Vanguard, this is the VTSAX: Vanguard Total Stock Market Fund, also available as a Vanguard Exchange Traded Fund (ETF) called VTI. In the TSP, you'll need to buy the C and S Fund.

- **total international stock market fund**. At Vanguard, this is the VTIAX: Vanguard Total International Stock Market Fund, also called ETF VXUS. In the TSP, it's the I Fund.

- **total bond fund**. At Vanguard this is the VBTLX: Total U.S. Bond Market Fund, also called BND as an ETF. In the TSP, it's the F or G fund.

These funds cost just pennies a year on thousands of dollars invested. With these funds you own over 5,000 of the best businesses around the world in dozens of countries. Your bond funds earn interest on thousands of short- and long-term government and corporate bonds.

If you want to recreate the VTSAX fund in the TSP, a market capitalization-weighted index fund, hold a 4x multiple of the C Fund relative to your S Fund. The 4x multiple is because the 500 companies in the C Fund are worth approximately 4x the thousands of companies in the S Fund.

For example, if you have 15 percent allocated to your S Fund, your C Fund should have 60 percent. Another option is 20 percent S fund, 80 percent C Fund. Any 4:1 ratio of C Fund to S Fund will recreate VTSAX in your TSP.

You can test any asset allocation to see your expected returns on a site like Portfolio Visualizer. By keeping it simple, you can minimize the chances of selecting a bad or overly complicated portfolio.

Keeping it simple can also help if you suffer from "analysis paralysis." This paralysis comes from over analyzing or becoming overwhelmed by your investment choices. I recommend starting with the "Bogleheads" Three-Fund Portfolio, as described above. The Bogleheads are fans of the investment philosophy of the founder of Vanguard, John "Jack" Bogle.

The Three-Fund Portfolio is a great place to start and finish. The portfolio is simply 34 percent total US stock market fund, 33 percent total international stock market fund, and 33 percent total bond fund. If you think the bond allocation is a bit high, like I do, adjust as you see fit. The Bogleheads Wiki website has an excellent collection of simple and easy asset allocations that you can implement quickly in your portfolio.

The important thing to focus on is not making speculative bets. Stick to low-cost passive index funds for the majority of your investment portfolio. If you feel like making risky investments, make sure you have first built a solid foundation of index funds.

If you do feel like making a speculative bet on a particular stock or cryptocurrency, I recommend using no more than 5 percent of your net worth. Protecting yourself from loss is much more important than swinging for the fences to try to hit a "home run" investment. Stick to the consistent base hits, rather than going for the home runs so you avoid an accidental strike-out.

ASSET ALLOCATION

So what should your asset allocation be? This is a complicated question, but in general, a reasonable mix of US stocks, international stocks, and bonds should be fine.

Begin with the TSP Lifecycle Fund that matches the year when you will be 60 years old. So if you were born in 2005, the L2065 fund is a good place to start. Or you could use the Vanguard LifeStrategy Growth Fund as an example, which has a mix of 80 percent stocks and 20 percent bonds in the fund.

The best way to build the asset allocation that's right for you is to continue to learn about the various recommended asset allocations. I included additional resources on this topic in the back of the book.

After doing all the research, like I have, you will probably do just fine with an 80 percent stock, 20 percent bond portfolio. In the TSP, this could look like:

- C Fund 64 percent
- S Fund 16 percent
- G Fund 10 percent
- F Fund 10 percent

Or at Vanguard you could own:

- VTSAX 40 percent
- VTIAX 40 percent
- VBTLX 20 percent

There is no way to know what the optimal asset allocation will be until we have 20/20 hindsight. It is much more important to save and invest your money than to get the perfect asset allocation.

My portfolio for the past few years has consisted of 70 percent US stocks, 25 percent international stocks, and 5 percent bonds. Is this the most correct answer? Probably not, but it's also probably not the most wrong one. I can comfortably stick to this allocation through good markets and bad, trusting that some years will be good, some will be bad, but in the end, I'll come out ahead.

CAN YOU BEAT OR TIME THE MARKET?

There are two schools of thought when it comes to investing:

1. I think I can beat the market or time it.

2. I think some people can beat the market some of the time, but I'm probably not one of them. I understand that timing the market takes skill, time, and luck—three things I probably don't have. Even if I could beat the market, this market-beating strategy is often only apparent in hindsight. Additionally, market-beating strategies can be expensive, require frequent trading, and can induce a lot of stress. I want to keep my investments low-cost and low-stress.

Timing the market is certainly *possible*. Especially once. You can have that gut feeling that tells you to sell everything in February 2020 and watch the market crater during the COVID-19 pandemic a month later. But will you then buy at the bottom, on March 20?

To time the market, you must be right twice: both when you sell *and* when you buy. It's almost impossible to get both of those dates right. According to a study by Fidelity, missing the 50 best return days of the market from 1980 to 2020 reduced investor returns by 93 percent! You don't want to be on the sidelines and miss those days due to market timing.

There certainly are investors who can beat the market. Warren Buffett is the classic example, but there are many others. But even Buffett understands that passive, index-fund investing usually beats the best active managers.

Buffett once bet a group of hedge fund managers $1 million that, minus fees, an S&P 500 index fund (the Vanguard fund VFIAX) would beat their average annual return. The original bet was supposed to be for a ten-year period, but by year eight, the hedge funds called it off because they were losing so badly. From 2008–2016 the expensive hedge funds returned an average of 2.2% percent while the low-cost S&P 500 index fund returned 7.1% percent. Buffett's bet once again proved the wisdom of low-cost, passive, index investing.

As a reminder, you are not Warren Buffett. Most of the people who can beat the market work on Wall Street and get paid lots of money to research, analyze, and process information about investments for 80 hours a week or more. You don't have the time, skill, or training to compete with them.

Even if you could beat the market this year, studies show that it's difficult to repeat the performance year after year.

In 2014, 86 percent of actively managed funds failed to beat the performance of their benchmark.

But don't despair. You don't have to beat the market to win at investing.

In summary:

- Index funds outperform active funds 90 percent of the time.
- Control what you can: costs, asset-allocation, and diversification.
- Keep your strategy LADS: low-cost, automatic, diversified, and simple.

If you don't want to take the time to figure out your asset allocation, then a Lifecycle Fund is perfect for you. After you have time to do a bit more research, you can switch to your own personal asset allocation plan. Then execute your plan with low-cost, simple, and diversified investments.

NON-RETIREMENT INVESTMENT ACCOUNTS

A discussion of investing while serving in the military would not be complete without addressing non-retirement investment accounts. Also known as "brokerage" or "taxable investment accounts," these are accounts that don't have special retirement tax advantage like the IRA or TSP.

These accounts allow you to own many investments, including stock index funds, bond index funds, certificates of deposit, and several others. Brokerage accounts are typically at large investment firms like Fidelity, Schwab, or Vanguard.

You can invest an unlimited amount of money into taxable investment accounts since unlike retirement accounts, they don't have annual contribution limits. A taxable investment account can be an excellent place to save additional funds after you exceed the annual contribution limits of your TSP and IRA retirement accounts.

If you are contributing the maximum annual contributions to your TSP and IRA, I recommend continuing to invest in your taxable investment account.

You can hold similar assets in your investment account that you hold in your TSP and IRA. For instance, you can hold the Vanguard Total Stock Market Index fund and Vanguard Total International Stock Market Index fund in your taxable account.

A taxable investment account has no penalties for accessing the funds before age 59 $\frac{1}{2}$. Taxable investment accounts are not as tax advantaged as retirement accounts. If you buy and hold funds for longer than one year, you will only be responsible for long-term capital gains tax when you sell. The long-term tax is significantly lower than short-term capital gains tax. Both taxes are based on your annual taxable income.

A COLLECTION OF INVESTING WISDOM

To close out the chapter on investing, I'll end with a collection of investing wisdom I learned over the years:

- Never invest in something you don't understand.

- By the time you hear about a trend, whether it's gold, cryptocurrency, or Beanie Babies, it's too late and you missed the opportunity. Don't suffer from FOMO (fear of missing out), and stick to your plan.

- If it's too good to be true, then it's probably not true.

- Anyone selling you an investment is probably not a fiduciary. They don't have your interests in mind, just their commissions.

- Someone who claims to be getting returns above the average should be considered suspicious. Anything that promises "guaranteed returns" is probably a scam.

- Make your investment purchases automatic and remove all emotion from your decisions. Invest regularly on a set schedule and don't ever change the schedule based on what the market is doing.

- Time *in* the market beats *timing* the market.

- Don't check your accounts every day. Don't even check them monthly. Let the money flow in and allow compounding to do its work. Check your accounts once every few months or once a year to rebalance them to your asset allocation.

- Boring is better. Low-cost, total-market index funds should be the 95+ percent core of your investing portfolio. Gamble or speculate with less than 5 percent of your portfolio.

UNIQUE ASPECTS
OF MILITARY FINANCES

You should now have a better understanding of investing while in the military. The LADS system should keep you from making costly investment mistakes. The TSP and Roth IRA are now the center of your investing portfolio.

Now let's talk about the unique aspects of military finances that civilians never have to deal with. In this chapter, we'll cover:

- Deployment
- Savings Deposit Program (SDP)
- Combat Zone Tax Exclusion (CZTE) Pay
- Extra Combat Zone TSP Contributions
- The Blended Retirement System
- Military Travel Hacking

DEPLOYMENT

Chances are good that you will deploy at some stage in your military career. Deployments are a great time to get in shape, learn about investing, cut your expenses to almost nothing, and boost your income.

Use deployment to maximize your investments, pay down debt, and put yourself in a better financial position than when you deployed. On my first deployment, I paid off my USAA Career Starter Loan two years early with the extra tax-free income I received.

While deployed, prioritize your Roth TSP and Roth IRA contributions, since your income will not be subject to federal income tax due to the Combat Zone Tax Exclusion. Roth contributions that are not taxed will grow untaxed and distribute after age 59 $\frac{1}{2}$ untaxed, giving you the chance to earn tremendous untaxed growth over the course of your life.

Another tip to reduce your expenses is let your auto insurer know you are storing your vehicle, and you should get a reduced rate. Turn off your cell phone plan and use a local SIM card or just use internet phone services to call home. Eat at the on base chow hall and don't waste money on snacks at the local Exchange.

If you are single and renting, move your stuff into storage and bank your BAH. If you bought your home, look at renting it out on sites like Airbnb while you are away. I earned over $10,000 renting out my condo on Airbnb over the course of three deployments.

Deployment can be the most financially beneficial time in your life. Use it to your advantage. Don't blow all your savings on a "tax-free" car from the Exchange or on other big expenses for things you don't really need.

COMBAT ZONE TAX EXCLUSION (CZTE)

When you deploy to a combat zone, your pay won't be subject to federal income tax. Even if you are only in a combat zone for one day, the entire month is tax-free. You pay no federal income tax during that month.

This benefit is known as Combat Zone Tax Exclusion (CZTE). You will still need to pay Social Security, which is listed as FICA on your Leave and Earnings Statement (LES), and Medicare tax. If your CZTE status is not on your LES, and you think you should be eligible, talk to your finance office immediately.

IRS-recognized combat zones change frequently, so do your research to see if you are in an eligible area. Some states will also exempt you from state income tax for the months when you're eligible for CZTE.

Remember the triple-tax benefit of CZTE pay when you contribute it to a Roth IRA or Roth TSP. CZTE pay goes into the account tax-free, grows tax-free, and withdraws tax-free after age 59 $\frac{1}{2}$.

EXTRA COMBAT ZONE TSP CONTRIBUTIONS

When you serve in a combat zone, you can make additional contributions to your Traditional TSP account beyond your normal annual limit. This is known as an annual addition limit and is an extra contribution to your elective deferral limit. In 2021, the annual addition limit is $58,000 and the elective deferral limit is $19,500.

Usually, you are better off investing any amount above the elective deferral limit into a taxable brokerage account or Roth IRA rather than the TSP. This is because while tax-free contributions to a Traditional TSP are withdrawn tax-free, the gains (or growth) on those contributions are taxed at the income tax rate.

In a taxable brokerage account, the investment gains are taxed at the capital gains tax rate. Capital gains tax rates are usually less than income tax rates.

SAVINGS DEPOSIT PROGRAM (SDP)

While deployed to a combat zone, you'll have access to special savings programs like the Savings Deposit Program (SDP). The SDP is a special savings account available through the Defense Finance and Accounting Service, or DFAS. It is only available to military personnel deployed to a combat zone.

You can deposit up to $10,000 into the account. The interest rate is 10 percent annually. You must wait 30 days once you deploy before you are eligible to contribute. Interest will continue to accrue for a few months after you leave the combat zone and then the entire amount will deposit into your checking account.

The SDP is one of the unique investment opportunities available to deployed troops. It is a great place to park your emergency fund savings while you are deployed. In case of emergency, you can request the funds be returned to your checking account. The funds should be deposited within three days.

While deployed, I recommend you max out your SDP. It can earn you an extra, risk-free, $1,000 per year.

THE BLENDED RETIREMENT SYSTEM

The Blended Retirement System, or BRS, is the military's new pension and retirement plan. If you joined the military after 2017, you are automatically enrolled in the BRS.

The legacy retirement system called "High-3" is only available if you joined before 2018. This military retirement system offered a 50 percent pension of base pay after completing 20 years of service but paid no benefits if you left the service before 20 years. This all-or-nothing approach to military retirement changed with the introduction of the BRS.

The BRS offers a smaller pension than the legacy High-3 plan. The BRS pension is calculated by multiplying your years of service by two to get the percentage of pay you'll receive. Multiply this percentage by the average of your highest 36 months of base pay to see your monthly pension amount.

For example, if you retire after 20 years as an O-5 making $10,000 per month for the last 36 months of your active-duty service, your formula is 40 percent (20 x 2) x $10,000 = $4,000 per month. Note that military pensions are inflation-protected by cost-of-living adjustments, or COLA.

To compensate for the smaller pension, the BRS adds an employer contribution match to the TSP. If you contribute 5 percent of your pay, the DoD will match your 5 percent. That's a guaranteed 100 percent return for the first 5 percent you contribute to the TSP.

The BRS also allows services to offer continuation bonuses at around the 10-year mark of service. This allows services to offer extra pay to critically needed service members at about the halfway point to a military retirement. Continuation bonuses add additional flexibility to your retirement savings under BRS.

The BRS 5 percent TSP contribution matching makes up for the reduced pension, especially since many service members do not serve for 20 years. An intelligent military investor can make up or exceed the reduced pension with savvy investing of the five percent TSP match throughout his or her career.

MILITARY TRAVEL HACKING

Thanks to the SCRA and MLA, military service members and their spouses have unique advantages over civilians when it comes to travel hacking. Several credit card companies and banks, including some with the best travel rewards cards, waive the annual fees on their top credit cards for military service members and their spouses.

This means you can get the Platinum Card from American Express or the Chase Sapphire Reserve card, which each cost civilians more than $500 a year, totally free.

At my peak travel hacking phase, my wife and I received over $7,000 a year in annual fee waivers. We had over 27 credit cards and did not pay an annual fee on any of them. We earned many free nights every year at Hilton and Marriott hotels and resorts just from being cardmembers. We also received thousands per year in free travel credit. We earned over three million points in three years, with a cash value of over $50,000. If you would like to learn more about military travel hacking, sign up for my free course at militarymoneymanual.com/umc3.

The advantages military service members have in the travel hacking game are unparalleled. The amount you can save on travel expenses can easily max out a Roth IRA every year, getting you closer to financial independence faster. Plus, you can enjoy the journey to FI a bit more at five-star hotels and in lie-flat seats. But never carry a balance, and don't play this game if you're struggling with debt.

PHILOSOPHY

OF FINANCIAL INDEPENDENCE

At some point on your journey to FI, you will ask yourself: "So, I reach FI . . . then what?" What's the point of saving and investing all this money?

The point is to buy yourself freedom and choices. When you achieve FI, you achieve freedom—freedom from having to go to work and the necessity of trading your time for money.

You can't buy yourself more time. At the extreme, you get about 100 years on this planet, and most people don't get that many. How you spend your days and years in the future is determined by the choices you make today.

If you choose, you can liberate your future-self from having to trade your time for money. You can focus on achieving FI rapidly, in less than 20 years, which means your future-self can focus on whatever interests you for the rest of your life.

Some of the concepts you should think about on the journey to FI are happiness, compounding returns, internal focus, and minimalism. By considering these concepts, you can be intentional about creating a better post-FI life for yourself.

HAPPINESS

Financial independence will not make you happy. Achieving a financial goal may provide a fleeting burst of happiness, but it does not last. Two aphorisms about happiness have stuck with me over the years.

The first is, "Wherever you go, there you are." If you are unmotivated, unhealthy, always late for appointments, and are unkind to others, you won't magically change when you reach FI.

If you are unhappy with who you are before FI, you probably won't be happy with the person you are after FI. Do not use your goal of FI as an excuse to delay self-improvement. FI is mostly automatic once you set the investment systems in place. You must practice continuous growth as a self-actualized human before you reach FI.

The second aphorism is, "How you spend your days is how you spend your life." Everyone, rich or poor, young or old, only has 24 hours in a day. Take away eight hours for sleep, and that leaves 16 hours in a day. Sixteen hours to do whatever you want. When you are working a full-time military job, the "fog of work" can blind you to what is truly important.

One popular lecture series at Yale University is "The Science of Well-Being." This course focuses on using the findings of psychological science to teach us how to be happier, feel less stressed, and flourish more. The popularity of the course tells us something—lots of people are looking to improve their well-being. Perhaps they are blind to what is truly important and are trying to rediscover it.

I've taken the course online. My biggest takeaway is that we think some things, like a good job, lots of money, power, or fame will make us happy, but in fact, they do not satisfy us when we get them. Harvard psychologist Dan Gilbert, the author of *Stumbling on Happiness*, refers to this as "miswanting." Most miswanting comes from the fact that we adapt to things easily. What was once a new exciting thing quickly becomes an old boring thing. This is also referred to as "hedonic adaptation." We adapt to the good things in life and crave more.

Some of the strategies suggested by Gilbert to overcome these issues are gratitude, kindness, social connection, and time affluence. FI can give you time affluence, or the ability to choose what you do with your time, but you must work on cultivating gratitude, kindness, and social connection for yourself.

For its part, the Yale course offers a series of "rewirements," or exercises to increase our own happiness and the happiness of those around us. These techniques are amazingly simple, but they can have a profound effect on your well-being and happiness. If you're interested, the course is available for free online.

COMPOUNDING RETURNS IN ALL THINGS

One concept I've grown to love is the idea that all the best things in life come from compounding returns. Whether it's a relationship, friendship, fitness, health, wealth, or a hobby: small, frequent investments over long periods of time grow into substantial amounts.

Take the example of investing an initial sum of $23,000 at 10 percent return over 40 years. At the end of 40 years, you're a millionaire. But here's the interesting thing; look at the breakdown of your million dollars: $23,000 is your initial investment, $92,000 is interest, and a full $925,000 is compound interest.

Most of your wealth is from the miracle of compounding interest, where your interest earned interest. And so it is in the rest of life. Most of your greatest experiences and joys in life come from small, frequent investments over long periods of time.

Take the time to invest daily in relationships that matter. Spend a few hours exercising every week. You'll be happier, healthier, and wealthier as a result. The little investment of time and energy in the things that matter to you will earn you dividends for the rest of your life.

Compounding interest works miracles in all facets of life, not just finance.

CONTROL WHAT YOU CAN, DON'T SWEAT THE REST

One of the most important lessons when it comes to personal finance and your journey to FI is to control what you can and not worry about the rest.

Psychologists refer to this mindset as an "internal locus of control," as opposed to an "external locus of control." People with an internal locus of control focus on the actions and outcomes they can control and influence. Those with an external locus focus on what they have no power over.

In investing, someone with an internal locus will focus on controlling costs, taxes, diversification, and costly mistakes. They will manage what they can: asset allocation, costs, and savings rate.

Someone with an external locus will focus on performance, timing the market, frequent trading to capture gains and minimize losses, and adjusting their asset allocation based on market indicators. But these are all elements of investing that you really have no control over. You don't know what the Federal Reserve Bank is going to do next week or how the newest trade deal with China will impact the market.

You can never increase your long-term returns without increasing your short-term risk. The market will do what the market will do. You are just a small fish in an exceptionally large ocean.

When you focus on what you can control, you can achieve a kind of peace with yourself and your decisions.

No one knows what the stock market will do in the next month, or year, or 10 years. But we do know that there has been no 25-year period in the past 100+ years during which the stock market declined.

Rather than thinking about whether small companies, large companies, or emerging markets will outperform in the next decade, simply select a diversified portfolio of low-cost stock and bond index funds and let the magic of compounding interest do its thing.

In addition to your savings rate, investment costs, and asset allocation, you can control the car you drive, the home you live in, the food you eat, the people you spend time with, the books you read, and the exercise you get—all things you have the power to decide.

Focus on the actions within your power and the other financial decisions you and your family can control. What the market does day-to-day, what impact world news will have on the economy, the outbreak of a new war somewhere, or whoever gets elected President—these things are out of your control, so do not sweat them.

Allow yourself to achieve financial zen.

LESS IS MORE:
EXPERIENCES (WITH PEOPLE) > THINGS

One more thing that I learned over the years: You get more pleasure from experiences, relationships, and quality goods than from cheaply made things and more stuff. Again, see Daniel Gilbert's book *Stumbling on Happiness* for the science behind experiences versus material things.

Allocate your money towards what really makes you happy long-term and don't waste it on things that give you only temporary happiness. I've found that having dinner with my family, quiet weekends at home with my wife, and a few beers with my friends are some of my greatest pleasures in life, and they cost almost nothing. The best things in life really are free. Just make sure the stuff you spend money on is worth it to you.

Buying tools, not toys, usually leads to more happiness. Tools enable you to do the work humans were meant to do. To play, to run, to ride, to swim, to move, to dance, to laugh. Toys are usually just cheap thrills or distractions that quickly fade away.

As the saying goes, when you have too many possessions, your possessions end up possessing you. Living a minimalist lifestyle isn't a deprived life. A life full of experiences with the people you love can be more enjoyable and fulfilling than surrounding yourself with possessions and toys. Even if you aren't ready to go full-on minimalist, you can still have plenty of toys and invest your way towards financial independence.

Time is our most valuable resource. Rich or poor, we only get 24 hours in the day. Anything that gives you more of your time back is worth looking into and possibly spending money on. But, even if you can free up more of your day, you can never buy more time.

When you reach financial independence, you'll be able to stop trading your time for money. It will give you the freedom to wake up and do whatever you want. That's the endgame.

> "The highest form of wealth is the ability to wake up every morning and say, 'I can do whatever I want today....' The ability to do what you want, when you want, with who you want, for as long as you want, is priceless. It is the highest dividend money pays."
>
> — Morgan Housel, *The Psychology of Money*

ADDITIONAL READING

I hope that this book inspires you to start your own journey towards financial independence. Here's a collection of recommended books, resources, and articles that helped me on my road to FI.

You can also find these and other recommended articles and links at militarymoneymanual.com/book-notes.

BOOKS ON INVESTING

This is $200 worth of books that will pay you back a thousand- or ten-thousand-fold.

- *The Psychology of Money* by Morgan Housel

- *Bogleheads Guide to Investing* by Mel Lindauer, Michael LeBoeuf, and Taylor Larimore

- *I Will Teach You to Be Rich* by Ramit Sethi

- *The Little Book of Common Sense Investing* by John C. Bogle

- *The Military Guide to Financial Independence and Retirement* by Doug Nordman

- *The Millionaire Next Door* by Thomas J. Stanley

- *A Random Walk Down Wall Street* by Burton Malkiel

- *The White Coat Investor* by James M. Dahle

- *The Simple Path to Wealth* by J. L. Collins

Each book offers a somewhat different perspective on investing and money management, but each almost always boils down to the same principles:

- Spend less than you earn.

- Insure against catastrophes.

- Invest in low-cost, passive index funds.

- Start saving as early as possible and compounding interest will work for you.

- Do not take on much debt and pay off debt ASAP.

- Create automated systems of saving, investing, and spending so you can spend time doing the things you love, not focused on money management.

BOOKS ON PERSONAL DEVELOPMENT

- *The Subtle Art of Not Giving a F*ck* by Mark Manson

- *The War of Art* by Steven Pressfield

- *Digital Minimalism* by Cal Newport

- *A Guide to the Good Life* by William Braxton Irvine

- *The 4-Hour Workweek* by Timothy Ferriss

- *Stumbling on Happiness* by Daniel Gilbert

WEBSITES ON FINANCIAL INDEPENDENCE

- **militarymoneymanual.com** – My website and where I post up-to-date content on achieving FI in the military.

- **the-military-guide.com** – Military financial topics focusing on how to set yourself up to live on the military pension.

- **gocurrycracker.com** – Real life couple that retired in their 30s. Tax minimization strategies and living overseas.

- **engaging-data.com** – Calculators and thoughts on achieving FI rapidly.

- **networthify.com/calculator** – An easy to use calculator to see how far you are from FI.

- **getrichslowly.org** – One of the oldest personal finance blogs with timeless content.

- **mrmoneymustache.com** – One of the original FI movement blogs that explains many of the FI concepts in an easy-to-read format.

- **mymoneyblog.com** – Daily updates on how to spend, earn, invest, and retire early.

- **madfientist.com** – Tax avoidance and strategies to help you retire even earlier.

- **portfoliovisualizer.com** – You can backtest—with real world data—any asset allocation to see your expected returns.

ABOUT THE AUTHOR

 I'm Spencer C. Reese, a US Air Force veteran who achieved financial independence. I started the website militarymoneymanual.com to share everything I know about military finance and investing with fellow service members of all ranks and branches.

You can learn more about me at:
militarymoneymanual.com/about

Introduce yourself or ask a question at:
militarymoneymanual.com/contact

I always reply.